Secrets
to
Survival

Secrets
to
Survival

"A MEMOIR"
BY
ANGELA MORRISON

iUniverse, Inc.
Bloomington

Secrets to Survival

iUniverse books may be ordered through booksellers or by contacting:

iUniverse
1663 Liberty Drive
Bloomington, IN 47403
www.iuniverse.com
1-800-Authors (1-800-288-4677)

ISBN: 978-1-4759-6090-7 (sc)
ISBN: 978-1-4759-6092-1 (hc)
ISBN: 978-1-4759-6091-4 (ebk)

Library of Congress Control Number: 2012921152

Printed in the United States of America

iUniverse rev. date: 11/19/2012

Dedication

Above all else, I would like dedicate this book to my Heavenly Father who has spared my life so many times. He has allowed Christ in me to lead, guide and protect me daily. I stand in awe at His unconditional love, grace and patience with me over the years when I've been stubborn or disobedient. All thanks, praise, glory and honour are due to Him.

This book is also a memorial to my precious mother and mentor, without whose strength of character, support, unconditional love, wisdom and great faith, I would not have survived. She taught me so much. I love, honour and thank her.

I also thank my husband, Owen, my children, family, friends and Madeleine who have supported and encouraged me to write about my secrets to survival. I sincerely thank Rowan for his help, knowledge, patience and support in helping me finalise this book. I appreciate and love them for their confidence in me.

Contents

Introduction

If your life resembles mine in any way, it will be like an enormous obstacle course, filled with daily challenges. In spite of your plans and goals, life keeps coming up with a barrage of set-backs, problems, stresses and seemingly impossible situations.

Have you been through some dark valleys in life's journey? Then this book is for you.

Are you in need of a dose of encouragement, hope and inspiration today? Well, I'm here to give you just that.

Imagine you are standing in front of my home, knocking on my door. I invite you in to share a coffee and a piece of my delicious Milk Tart with me. I want you to feel welcome and special, because that's what you are! Sit down and relax and let me share my secrets to survival with you.

I have endeavoured to make this a quick and powerful read that will make you laugh and cry as you hopefully identify with the poignant illustrations from true life situations woven into each chapter.

This is an account of my growing up as a politician's daughter and my first-hand experiences of the historical changes that took place in the pre and post-Apartheid era in South Africa. It is one of the most beautiful countries on earth but, sadly, has become one of the most dangerous places in the world to live, riddled with crime, poverty and Aids.

I was sexually molested at a very young age; I had a son with serious learning difficulties and who eventually became addicted to drugs after being on prescribed medication from the age of four; I survived losing family, my business, my home and possessions and was the victim of violent criminal attacks.

At the moment, I live in England. Coming from a country where the climate can be unbearably hot the majority of the time, the English find it very strange when I tell them how much I love the English weather. I enjoy the changes of the seasons which are so evident, bringing with them a freshness I find invigorating. It's an exciting adventure of learning and experiencing a different culture and new things every day. I feel so fortunate to have had this opportunity. Who knows how long I have left? After all, I'm over sixty years of age. I have to fit twenty years of quality living into ten years at this time of my life. I have, however, discovered that life has begun at sixty for me!

I was on an assignment in Dorchester recently when my client Edwina's niece visited her for the weekend. After settling her aunt down for the night, we sat chatting till the early hours of the morning. She questioned me a great deal about my family, general everyday life in South Africa and was curious about why I had moved to England. After our discussion, she asked me if I'd ever thought of writing about my experiences. I told her I had been writing for many years as a means of self-therapy. She then asked if she could read what I had written.

I felt my writing technique and general grammar were not of a good standard, as I wrote as I thought and felt in the moment. She read for a while before excusing herself and going to her bedroom. She returned and handed me a business card. She worked for a literary agency in London who looked for writers wanting to have their work published. Without her encouragement, I would have never written this book at all. That is now history and here I am today with a completed book!

It is my hope that, as you journey through the many differing topics in each chapter, you will be encouraged. You will probably cry and laugh as you read about some of the predicaments I have got myself into. My desire is that you will be encouraged, as you learn about my secrets to survival—which are so practical - to never give up.

Chapter 1

LIFE AS A POLITICIAN'S DAUGHTER

My parents met on the troop ship on which my mother's family were travelling from Mauritius to South Africa during the 2nd World War. My uncle was attending university in South Africa and had decided to settle there. He encouraged his family to immigrate to South Africa and begin a new life, much to the delight of his four sisters. My father was an Officer in the British Merchant Navy. It was love at first sight when he first met my beautiful, petite mother. Within three days, he had asked her to marry him. My grandfather was horrified. He promptly informed Dad that the family was going to settle in Durban and that, if my father still had the same intentions after the war, he would have to leave the Navy and be in a secure occupation on land before my Grandfather would give his consent to the marriage.

When the war ended, Dad's ship called in at Durban. Derrick Watterson was determined to marry the love of his life and to settle in South Africa. The couple had been corresponding for what had seemed like an eternity and, at last, the time had come for them to meet again. They became engaged during that visit. Dad returned to England. He was the eldest of twelve children, and an extremely bright, intelligent young man. He remained in active service until the end of the war. He resigned from the Navy and sorted out his family matters. He had had a very traumatic childhood and, being the eldest child, was forced to take on great responsibility for a man so young. His mother had married and divorced three times. This resulted in all the siblings being put into homes. Having completed his education, Dad joined the Navy. His much younger brothers and sisters were still in homes at the end of the war. Dad returned to England to establish a family home for his mother and his siblings. He bought a little restaurant to earn a living so that the Watterson clan could all to be together again. Throughout the years of the War and after its end, he never forgot or neglected his family in England. Dad taught us by example how important family life was and how a child should honour parents, no matter what kind of up-bringing they had been given. I never heard my father speak disrespectfully of his parents. After ensuring all was well with his family in England, he returned to South Africa to marry the lovely Maysie Rivalland on the 18th May, 1945.

The family grew rapidly. In 1946, my sister Vivienne was born followed by myself fourteen months later. Georgina arrived in 1950 and Donald in 1951. The family was living in a flat on the Berea in Durban. When their fourth child arrived, they bought a property perfectly suited to our family's needs in Umbilo, a neighbouring middle class suburb. It was a large house with a building in front of the property which accommodated Dad's business. For 58 years this was home to our large family.

Shortly after moving into the house, Dad was invited to join the local Council Association. His leadership skills soon became evident and, before long, he was voted onto the Durban City Council as Councillor for Umbilo. Mum although not happy about his decision to enter public life, nonetheless supported him. She was definitely the power behind the throne throughout his political career.

Being a discerning person, it didn't take Dad long to assess that some of the Councillors were deeply involved in corruption. I can remember my parents speaking late into the night about the appalling activities of some of his fellow Councillors. He had such high morals that the bribery and corruption which was rampant amongst some of the Council members and leaders abhorred him. When he came home from meetings, frustrated and angry at what was going on in the chambers, Mum would always be on hand to calm him down, to encourage him to hold his peace and wait for God to expose everything in His time. She was right. It wasn't long before a number of Councillors were arrested for bribery and corruption. To our amazement, even the Mayor of Durban was sent to prison.

Throughout his life, Dad was well known for his straight-talking and soon got a reputation for being a person who did not suffer fools gladly. As his child, I found this part of my life difficult as Dad always seemed to be involved in some controversial issue or another. Growing up, I learned to keep my relationship to Dad to myself, shielding even from my close friends. Obviously, people were always very curious about that part of our family life. I personally tried to avoid being drawn into any discussions about Dad's public life and the controversial situations he constantly seemed to get himself into.

During the years that followed, Mum gave birth to twins, a boy and a girl. Sadly, she lost the girl at birth. Little Derrick was treasured by the whole family who rejoiced that that he had been spared. Not too long after Derrick's arrival in this world, my sister Valerie was born. She was a very gentle, kind girl, so much like Mum in character. Dad was the archetypal stiff-upper-lip Englishman, seldom showing his emotions, except when he was provoked to anger. Mum, by contrast was the typically demonstrative French type, warm and lovingly affectionate. Their widely differing temperaments meant that the children would sooner confide in Mum rather than Dad. Yet, strangely enough, as we got older, we began to confide in our father more as he mellowed and became more approachable and tolerant in his old age.

Life growing up in the Watterson home was not easy. The strict discipline Dad brought from his naval career played a decisive part in his handling of his large family. We were all assigned our duties and seldom neglected them for fear of punishment. I suppose having such a large family necessitated this strictness. Despite his unflinching enforcement of domestic law and order, Dad showed a distinct softening towards my brother Donald when he arrived on the scene after three daughters. This on-going show of favouritism was a constant source of annoyance to the three of us. We nick-named our brother 'Little Lord Fauntleroy'. Dad had this English 'thing' about boys somehow being entitled to many more privileges than girls. There was no doubt that

Donald, being the eldest, was the more favoured of the two sons. Later on in life, I could see an analogy between Donald and the Joseph of the Old Testament in the Bible. In Genesis 37, Joseph's father, Jacob, made his favourite son the famous 'coat of many colours'. That proved to be the straw that broke the camel's back for Joseph's siblings. This demonstration of favouritism by Jacob caused his other sons to hate Joseph and to plot getting rid of their brother. Thankfully, the siblings in the Watterson household never went to that extreme! However, his older sisters made Donald's life a misery when Dad wasn't around, teasing him relentlessly. Children can be very cruel when faced with rejection or jealousy, and we were no different. In hindsight, I see the damage the favouritism caused both to Donald and the rest of us. It had far-reaching effects throughout his and our lives. Having grown up in that damaging atmosphere with its detrimental effect on our family, I vowed, with God's help, to never make a Joseph out of any of my children.

When my brothers' wives gave birth to sons, they were given a Kruger Rand by their father-in-law. When we girls had sons, we received nothing. We were annoyed and hurt at the time but we soon got over it. Years later, Dad changed his way of thinking and apologised, telling us we had been good daughters and had made him very proud. His grand-daughters were given a Kruger Rand for their 21st Birthdays . . . his way of saying "sorry". He was very generous in enabling all of us to purchase our first homes when we married, making no differentiation between the sons and daughters, for which we were all very grateful.

In 1968, Dad was elected Deputy Mayor of Durban. This was a difficult time for my dear mother, who discovered at the age of 45, that she was expecting her eighth child. During the final months of her pregnancy, as Mum couldn't attend to her official duties as Deputy Mayoress, I accompanied my father to some of his functions in Mum's place. Chantal was born when I was 20 years old. Dad was so proud of her and strutted around 'like a cat with seven tails', cradling my baby sister in his arms, showing her off to everyone. After his having entered politics, he rarely showed this softer side of his character. I loved seeing him more vulnerable, gentle and affectionate—here was the Dad I remembered as a small child.

While Dad was on the City Council, as a representative of the United Party, the official opposition to the Apartheid Nationalist Government, he was elected to Provincial Council. This meant he had to spend a great deal of time in Pietermaritzburg away from home. Before long, he was elected to the Executive Committee, the highest leadership body in the Province under the Administrator. He held two portfolios: Hospitals and Local Government. As Executive of Local Government, an extremely powerful position, he oversaw the wonderful opportunity of being able to elect non-whites into local government positions.

Because of his outspokenness against the ruling Apartheid regime, he was constantly targeted by right wing Afrikaans groups and received many threatening phone calls and letters. He was referred to many times in these as "a Kaffir lover", "Kaffir" being an extremely derogatory name for the Black African people of our country.

The evening after Dad had been very blunt in an afternoon meeting, Mum received an anonymous telephone call. The caller had a very broad Afrikaans accent and said, "We know your husband is away. He's doing too much for these Kaffirs. He is bringing shame to the white people of this land. We are coming to kill you and your children."

Mum replaced the receiver. She calmly gathered us together, like mother hen gathering her chicks. She prayed with us, telling us to get under our beds and stay there until she told us it was safe to come out. There were no mobile phones in those days and Dad did not have a telephone in his new apartment. She couldn't reach him to tell him of the threat or ask his advice. She couldn't even phone the police. Dad was well known for the political stand he took and the police force was an arm of the Apartheid Government. They would not have helped us anyway. Thankfully, the threat wasn't carried that night, but the seeds of fear had been sown in us from a very early age because of the constant threats made to Dad and the family. Mum's faith and prayers carried us through those long frightening years.

Families would secretly come to see Dad at night for fear of being seen entering our property in daylight. They knew, and so did we, that he was under constant surveillance. Most of these callers came to ask Dad to help them with race classifications. Under the race classification system of those days of Apartheid, often one or more members of a family were classified as "white" and other members as belonging to another race. Under the Group Areas Act, they were not permitted to live under the same roof. This inhumane system meant families were split up and members forced to live in the areas allocated to their race group. Those trying to live together as families were often reported by neighbours or by members of their own families who disapproved of their mixed racial relationship. They would be arrested and charged under the Group Areas Act. This meant they could be imprisoned immediately for 30, 60 or 90 days . . . without a trial! We heard of many instances where front doors were broken down and the 'offending' partner was arrested and taken away in the middle of the night. Dad was acquainted with many unfortunate people who were categorised and penalised by this obnoxious legislation.

This imprisonment period didn't only apply to the Group Areas Act it also applied to any indiscretion they believed deserved this punishment. In those days all Black Africans were forced to carry special identity books on their person's at all times. They called these books their 'Passes'. They could be arrested for simply not carrying them at all times. If they were ever stopped in the street by the police, and especially after curfew which if I remember rightly was 10 p.m. they would also be arrested for 30, 60 or 90 days.

Dad had an employee, who disappeared for two months and both Dad and the man's family thought he had been murdered. It was a very distressing time for his poor family and we as a family were very upset at the loss of this good man. There was great jubilation when he returned. He had been detained for failing to have his identity book on him. He worked for a further forty five years for the family.

The authorities had the cruellest way of classifying people in different race groups and when Dad heard how these inspections were carried out, he went to see for himself. The people being classified would stand in front of the authorities for a physical examination. The size of their lips and noses were noted, their mouths were peered into and a pencil was poked and prodded into their hair to see if the pencil slipped through or got stuck. While these so-called experts made their assessment, they would pass derogatory remarks in Afrikaans, which most of these unfortunate people understood perfectly.

My father was devastated as he could not believe anyone could treat another human being so cruelly. These unfortunate people would come to him as a last resort, knowing he would never turn them away and would always fight for their cause.

The Apartheid Government hierarchy would often say to him, "Derrick, you are a very clever man. We need you on our side. Why are you wasting your time and efforts on these people? We would give you a Cabinet position if you'd only join us." This infuriated him as he had fought Apartheid all his life and there was not the slightest possibility of him ever crossing the floor. He couldn't believe the lengths they went to in their endeavours to stop him. Most of the classification cases he fought against were reversed so that families were at least reunited. He believed the authorities gave into his requests just to get rid of him, knowing he would never give up.

He never turned anyone away. One Sunday morning, an elderly lady phoned Dad weeping. She told him her dog had died and she had no-one to help her bury it. Immediately, Dad got the spade out of the shed and called my younger brother to accompany him. Off they went to bury the dog.

He had a great love and respect for the elderly and would go out of his way to help them. My parents were both extremely generous and hospitable. They were always inviting people for meals or giving them food parcels or monetary gifts to alleviate their plight. Throughout our lives, I remember Mum cooking for the poor in our area every week. As children, we would complain about how much our parents were always doing for others. Even when she went on holiday, Mum would deep-freeze the food for weeks in advance saying, "The poor still need to eat whilst I'm away enjoying myself . . . we can't be selfish." Whenever we complained, she always replied, "This is part of what being a public servant is all about my child. They trust us and we have to be there for them." What a far cry from the politicians of today!

Dad was later asked to stand for Parliament. He couldn't speak Afrikaans as he had been educated in Britain, but, being the determined man he was, he decided to teach himself the language. As so many of the Members of that day addressed Parliament in Afrikaans, he had to understand what they were saying and be able to answer them . . . he had no choice but to learn the language. It was hilarious listening to him practising his Afrikaans. We would stand outside his study door, giggling at his pronunciation. His vocabulary was faultless but his pronunciation and accent were atrociously English. Even after living in South Africa for almost sixty years, he never lost his English accent.

Dad's election campaign ran like clockwork with his efficient and hard-working wife at his side. The people in our area loved Mum. She was always so warm, friendly and kind to everyone and was never too busy to stop and chat with whoever she met in the malls or streets. As children, we hated going into public places with her as we knew we were going to have to stop constantly for Mum to chat to people all along the route between home and our destination, particularly in the area we lived. Many people suggested Dad should move to a more affluent area, but Dad wouldn't hear of it. He loved Umbilo and its people, they were all so loyal to him and in turn he supported them and all the local shops and businesses in the area. He actually did buy properties elsewhere but never moved to any of them.

We were trained in all aspects of campaigning as we grew older. It wasn't easy being part of the family of a politician, especially as a teenager, seeing my friends socialising and having fun while I had to help Mum and Dad with the election campaigns. I was always more involved in Dad's political life, than my other siblings which pleased him. I was a member of the United Party Youth in our area and eventually became secretary.

He won his Parliamentary seat, which meant acquiring another home in Cape Town as Parliament convened there. He now had a platform to have some real clout.

In 1981, the Government proposed the building of an enormous new Industrial site up the North Coast of what was then known as Natal, on the East coast of South Africa. When this proposed development came up for discussion, Dad went to Cape Town for these talks. He told the authorities in no uncertain terms that they should not even contemplate a move of this nature and size. It would involve the migration of millions of people to the area without any provision of the proper facilities to accommodate them. They needed adequate housing, security, schools, hospitals and social facilities . . . this to him was just plain common sense. His reasons for opposing that proposed development really riled the radical right wing Afrikaans groups. At that time, these groups had begun using violence as a means of stopping any progress towards Democracy. Terror tactics were rampant and there many murders and bombing incidents at that time.

A few nights later, Father was awoken by a phone call in his Cape Town residence at 1.30am. A reporter he knew well was calling to ask him for a statement about the bombing of his home in Durban that had just taken place. He was horrified and feared for Mum and my two sisters who were asleep in the house at the time. He phoned home immediately. Mum answered. The bombing had occurred some ten minutes earlier at the business premises at the bottom of the property and not at his home as the caller had said. The family was in such a state of shock trying to grasp what had happened that they hadn't had time to call him. Thankfully no one was injured.

Following the bombing, extensive repairs to the building had to be carried out. As soon as they were completed, Dad and other colleagues resumed meeting there with Black leaders and other opposition politicians, developing a blue print for change in South Africa. When it was completed the paper was called "The Indaba."—The word Indaba means a gathering of the Zulu leaders to discuss important issues concerning the people. Sadly, many of the changes agreed to in those meetings were not taken on board when change eventually did come about.

While so many ANC and members of other parties went into exile or received overseas funding, some faithful black leaders remained in South Africa throughout those years in an attempt to reach a peaceful settlement through negotiation. For their many years of hardship and patience, they were never accorded the honour and gratitude due to them when South Africa became a Democracy. I believe it was their influence over the Zulu people and their many years of negotiations that prevented what could have been a bloodbath, particularly in KwaZulu Natal. The new democracy was nick-named the "Rainbow Nation". However, the benefits that came with the change were not to be enjoyed by all race groups as the title might have suggested. Under Apartheid, Blacks, Indians and Coloured people were called "non-whites". Under the new democracy, the whites, Indians and Coloureds did not benefit from the change. The new laws of Affirmative Action only afforded benefits to the Black people in the workplace.

In 1987, Father said he felt it was time for him to retire. We all laughed and wondered how long that would last. He nearly drove Mum crazy giving his expert opinions on how to run the home which she had successfully managed without his assistance for some fifty years. He had been so active all his life that he found retirement boring.

We were right . . . retirement only lasted a few months and he was approached to stand for the Durban City Council once again. Within months of winning his seat, he was elected Mayor of Durban. Mum made a most gracious and elegant Mayoress. He was no sooner elected Mayor when he was thrown into yet another controversial issue . . . that of opening the previously "Whites only" Durban beaches to all race groups.

Under the Apartheid regime, amenities were segregated and Black, Indian and Coloured people were allocated their own beaches and other facilities. On this occasion, Dad opposed the opening of the beaches to all races for the moment . . . and for very practical reasons. Being a man of vision, he realised that preparation had to be made for matters like security, ablution facilities and transport to accommodate the enormous influx of millions of extra people flocking to the beaches. The existing facilities were totally inadequate and these changes would take time to put into place.

At the time of the beach controversy, I was in hospital after having just undergone surgery. Oblivious of whose daughter I was, the women in my ward were discussing my father whose photograph was splashed over all the newspapers. I wondered how they would they react if they knew who I was. Strangely enough, they never asked my opinion on the matter. I never volunteered it as I listened amused at their conversations on the matter. I dreaded that newspaper vendor coming in every morning and afternoon. Much to my relief, they never spoke adversely about the stand he had taken, so it didn't bother me too much.

Eventually, the day came for the Council to vote for or against the beaches opening to all the race groups. Father used his casting vote as Mayor to stop it being passed, until the correct facilities were put in place. At last it was over . . . or so I thought. My peace was short lived. I was dozing off that afternoon when I heard one of the ladies say, "A big black car has stopped in front of the hospital. I wonder who it could be. Oh, it's the Mayor! He's coming into the hospital!" They had recognised him immediately from the photographs which had been all over the media. I cringed and pulled the covers up, pretending to be asleep. "Oh Dad" I thought, "How could you do this to me?" He walked in the ward and came up to my bed smiling and asked, "How's my girl today?"

The women were shocked and whispered together throughout his visit. The moment he walked out, they couldn't wait to ask me why I had never mentioned my association with him. I just shrugged my shoulders and said, "You never asked my opinion and you would never understand." Because we had lived such a public life, not divulging our relationship to him was the only way to keep our privacy and live normally. Anyway, to me he was just my Dad.

After the advent of democracy in South Africa in 1994, Dad was very disappointed at some of the changes that came about. Nepotism, fraud and corruption were rife. The Affirmative Action law destroyed many flourishing businesses in a short while. He was too tired to fight anymore. He did, however, recognise and commend those who brought positive changes of which there were many. He had done all he could do and was now ready to retire and spend time with his family.

Shortly before his death, a cocktail party was held at the city hall for the past Mayors of Durban. Dad was invited. They were all seated when the Zulu King arrived. As he made his entrance, everyone rose to their feet as a sign of respect. He caught sight of Dad who was now looking old and frail. He walked over to him, put his hand on his shoulder and said, "You, old man, you don't stand for me." Mum told us later how the tears ran freely down Dad's cheeks as the King greeted them warmly. This was very unusual for Dad as he was always so composed.

At the age of 83, he began having health problems. One day, after visiting him in hospital, we had no sooner arrived home when the Matron telephoned to say that father was missing from the hospital and couldn't be found anywhere. I couldn't believe what I was hearing. We raced back to the hospital to find him standing outside the hospital in his brown towelling knee-length gown and leather slippers, clutching his holdall. His bare lily white legs protruding from his dressing gown were a sight to behold! He had had enough of hospitals and doctors and had decided to go home. He had simply packed his bag and walked out. How could we be cross with him? Mum and I couldn't stop giggling on the drive home . . . he looked so funny.

Shortly after this, he underwent further tests. The consultant recommended an immediate amputation of his leg, as gangrene had already set in. Father refused saying, "I came into this life with two legs and I'm going out the same way." After many more tests and much deliberation, another consultant was called in for a second opinion. He told Mum that Dad had numerous serious health problems and that he would probably live a maximum of six to eight weeks. He advised against amputation given his overall health condition. He recommended Dad go home and spend the rest of his life peacefully with his family. Dad insisted on knowing the truth. He knew he was dying, but was nonetheless delighted to go home to his familiar surroundings and to be able to spend his last days with his family. I went to stay with them to help Mum look after him.

Dad had put so much work and effort into his earthly life but I was worried about his spiritual life. I needn't have worried as I discovered his Heavenly Father loved him much more than I ever could have and had been ministering to him during this time. He had the television tuned to a Christian channel for about three days and was watching its programmes constantly. I was surprised because I had never seen him watching this sort of programme . . . in fact, previously he would probably have been highly critical of them. Nonetheless, I was amused at God's sense of humour, as it was quite a radical Christian channel and the lady preacher had 'pink dyed hair'. He seemed mesmerised by what he was watching and hung onto her every word. During that time, we had a private talk and I voiced my fears and feelings about his salvation to him. His steel blue eyes looked straight into my eyes as he said, "I know Jesus the Nazarene, Angie. Don't worry, my girl. We will be in Heaven together". Dad remained active until three days before he died. On the 17th December, 2003, he left his study for the last time after paying his monthly bills.

I found it difficult to believe and accept that this strong man, who had played such an integral part in all our lives, was going to be leaving us soon. Nothing threatens our courage more than the thought of losing a loved one. I knew only my trust in God would get me through this. Death takes enough as it is, so I was not going to allow the thief who is Death to take my courage as well. I needed it to carry on and deal with the fact that Dad would no longer be with us soon. We as a family needed the strength to comfort and support each other. My courage grew as I took hold of God's promises and I began to see death as a mere mile-post for Dad on his journey to the loving arms of his heavenly Father. I began to focus on the goodness of God, thanking and praising Him for Dad's life. As a result, I felt a peace that passed my human understanding and an assurance that all would be well. There was always one or more of the family at his side, seeing to his every need as well as talking, singing, praying or reading from his well-worn Navy Bible.

At 8am on Saturday the 20th December, 2003, Dad died with Mum and his children at his bedside. I felt, as did my siblings, extremely privileged to have been there with him.

I remember shortly after his death, a friend saying, "I'm sorry you've lost your Dad." My reply was, "Don't be sorry, I haven't lost him. I know exactly where he is." To many this may sound rather bold or even arrogant, but as a believer in Jesus Christ, I had an absolute assurance of the truth of God's Word in Acts 16. 30:31 which says, "Believe on the Lord Jesus Christ and you will be saved, you and your household." 2 Corinthians 5:8 says, "So we are always confident, knowing that while we are at home in the body we are absent from the Lord. For we walk by faith not by sight. We are confident, yes, well pleased rather to be absent from the body and to be present with the Lord." Dad had believed in the Lord Jesus Christ and now, absent from his body, he was in the presence of His Lord and Saviour. Death for Dad was the exit by which he had left this physical, temporal state of limitations, sickness and grief and he had entered a new dimension of spiritual and eternal peace.

No one I've ever known loses a loved one without thinking, "If only I had done this for him or that for her" or "If only I'd said this or hadn't said that." I was no different. Such guilt complicates grief. Our loved ones who are now living in God's perfect love in Heaven would never want us to torment ourselves with guilt or regrets. My greatest comfort was realising that my father who loved me would never want me to be tormented or unhappy. One day, I visualised myself digging a grave and burying all the negative thoughts and regrets I had felt about Dad. I imagined him standing next to me saying "Throw it in the grave, get rid of it, my girl! I am so happy here and I want you to be happy too." What freedom this brought me!

The family wanted to keep the funeral arrangements private but, that was an impossibility given his many years in public life. As Dad had never attended any church of his own, Mum had his funeral at her church. It was an honour for a non-Catholic to be allowed this privilege.

Mum had been a devout Catholic all her life—a pillar of the church so to speak. Dad had agreed to have us brought up as Catholics when they married. Mum ensured that we attended Catholic schools and regular Catechism classes. Every evening Mum would summons us to prayer time. We would kneel around a linen chest in the sitting room for evening prayers. As a child they seemed never ending and we seemed to pray for everyone. If Dad was there he would sit in his chair observing but never partaking. Before Mum got her driver's licence Dad was the one who got us all up for Mass every Sunday morning driving us to and from church. The only time Dad ever came to church with us was for our First Holy Communion, Mass, our Confirmation service, their wedding anniversaries or the usual Christenings, weddings and funerals.

For these reasons we were very surprised at the pomp and ceremony afforded him for his funeral. The then Archbishop of Durban—Archbishop Denis Hurley, the most significant South African Catholic leader of recent decades attended, giving his appreciation of Dad's admirable service to his country. Five priests who had known Dad during his public life had volunteered to officiate at the service as well. For a non-churchgoer, he got quite a send-off!

The service had just started when the roar of motor cycle engines drowned out the priest's voice. We all looked at each other in bewilderment. Police were circling the church grounds on their motor cycles. Then all went silent. The priest stopped speaking. Everyone turned around. Dr Mangosuthu Bhutelezi, leader of the Inkatha Freedom Party and his entourage appeared through the door at the back of the church. They had come to pay their last respects to their faithful old friend. In true traditional African time, they were late! As Dr Bhutelezi gave his eulogy, he spoke of Dad's brave stand for a new South Africa over five decades and honoured him, calling him a true African. He shared many of the changes Dad brought about during his lifetime. Speaking of their friendship, he said ending, "I deem it an honour to be called a friend of Derrick, my true friend." We, his children, were very proud to have heard our dear father honoured by so many people that day.

God has His unique plans for people. We are all unique to Him and to each other. When I reflect on that part of my life, I realise that, during those years, I had learned much about honouring parents, obedience and a sense of duty that no book could have taught me. I am thankful and proud to have been a politician's daughter!

SURVIVING SEXUAL
MOLESTATION AS A CHILD

My earliest memories as a small child were of being tormented by nightmares and terrifying images. These images would come in different forms but the subjects were always the same. I was so disturbed not knowing what they meant or why I kept having the nightmares. One of the most vivid was of people dressed in white, their seemingly large faces looming towards me. I know now that they were the district surgeons examining me. I also remember standing at the front door of our family home with very tall policemen dressed in brown uniforms looking down at me as they questioned me.

Another memory was of being in a room filled with dark wooden furniture, and of men dressed in black, asking me questions. Their faces always looked very stern. I was frightened by them. Looking back now, I know the setting of this disturbing memory was a courtroom.

These dreams and images recurred throughout my life for many years. Then, I didn't know why I was having them or what they meant. When I was young, children never questioned or their parents or adults or argued with them. Mention of abuse and sexual subjects was deemed taboo and any conversation on these topics was discouraged or avoided. Today, children generally have far more open communication with their parents and adults than I ever had as a child. For as long as I can remember, I always felt I had done something very wrong. I never knew how it was that I had erred and could never make sense of the nightmares and images that so troubled me. I grew up tormented with such fear and guilt that I was wetting my bed until I was 12 years of age. My siblings teased me endlessly about this. Children can be very cruel to each other, oblivious of the rejection and hurt they are inflicting.

My bed-wetting wasn't due to a medical problem or because I slept too deeply. I was simply too scared to go to the bathroom alone. I would wake my sister up, much to her annoyance, and plead with her to come with me to the bathroom. On the odd occasion, she would come with me, but most often, she refused so I had no option but to go back to my bed. I would will myself to sleep, hoping I would forget that I needed to go to the bathroom. The obvious result was that I wet the bed! I hated having this problem . . . it was so demeaning and I was so ashamed. Mum was always so kind and helpful, covering up for me in an endeavour to spare me the humiliation.

I was haunted by the troubling images and fear until 1976 when I was 28 years old. Early that morning, my husband Vernon had left to go on a business trip to Cape Town for a few days. I was about to take out girls to school and then go on to work. I had opened the front driveway gates to our home at about seven o'clock in the morning. After putting my daughters in the car, parked in the garage, I got into the driver's seat and opened the window about to start the car. Suddenly, there was a man standing beside my car! "I want a job!" he said. I was so shocked and my heart started pounding. How on earth had I not seen or heard him? He must have been watching me and planned his moves very quickly. I felt trapped with this man standing intimidatingly at the car window. I had a great deal of cash in my handbag, lying on the passenger seat beside me. I had withdrawn Vernon's salary in cash the night before. The man's eyes searched the interior of the car and then fell on my bag. I could not afford to lose it, with all our money in it.

I slammed the car into reverse and accelerated. The man had closed the driveway gates, to block my escape route. Obviously, he had done this to trap me in the garage and rob me. I crashed the car through the gates and ripped them off their hinges. They fell onto the sidewalk in front of our home. The man panicked, jumped over the wall and ran away. The children and I were shocked but relieved we were unharmed.

This incident opened a floodgate of memories—horrible, painful memories that would plagued my mind over the following days. I could not understand why, after all these years, these memories began to torment me so suddenly.

After the attempted robbery, my mind dwelt on many distressing images. I remembered a family friend of my parents who had very often exposed himself to me. He had tried to touch me inappropriately from when I was five until I was almost 12 years old. I hadn't thought about this man for many years. Now, I found myself recalling him with such anger. He had stolen my childhood from me. He had deprived me of what should have been the happiest, carefree years of my life. Throughout my childhood I had been filled with fear, guilt and torment together with abnormal anxiety and such shame. I felt such bitterness and hatred towards him and was consumed by thoughts of revenge. This was not me! These thoughts were so out of character! What was happening to me? Was I going mad? Had these things really happened to me?

I felt I was losing my mind. I made an appointment to see our family doctor. He had been a close friend of the family since I was about five years old. I told him everything that had happened to me during those years of abuse. I shared how I had become obsessed with these awful thoughts and memories since the attempted robbery two days earlier. He listened patiently and then quietly explained the strange complexities of the human mind. He told me how a shock or trauma can often suddenly release memories of the past. I knew that my abuser was also one of his patients. My doctor pleaded with me to identify the man. He was very concerned that he may still be abusing this other children. I refused to divulge my abuser's name.

After our talking for almost an hour, he asked me to sit in the waiting room as he needed to make a telephone call. After about ten minutes, he called me back into his office and said, "Angela, I have just spoken to your mother. You are not crazy, my girl. In fact, I don't know how you have lived normally all these years." He then told me that something really serious had happened to me before he had befriended our family. For all the years since then, he had been unaware of this. Had he known, he would have spoken to me about it before. He gently broke the awful news that I had been sexually abused when I was three and a half years old. This traumatic event had happened before the family friend had started abusing me for all those years. My doctor told me my mother was waiting at home for me . . . she would tell me everything.

He then explained to me that the subconscious mind is like a filing cabinet where every thought, word and deed from one's life is stored. This part of our mind cannot differentiate between right and wrong thoughts until they rise to the conscious mind and one has a chance to think them through rationally. In my particular situation, it would be a case of my acknowledging that I had been three and a half years old, just a child. I had not been responsible for what had happened to me . . . I was the victim. Only after doing that, would I be able to understand and put the whole episode into perspective. I had never gone through that process. I was now 28 years old. It had been a long time to have had to carry the fear, the guilt and the shame. For the first time in so many years, I began to feel a sense of relief. Now that I knew I wasn't crazy, these images which had haunted me for so long finally meant something. I began to understand why I had felt the way I had. My doctor reassured me he would get me professional help as soon as possible as I obviously needed it but, he said, my priority was to get to my mother.

Mum was waiting anxiously on the patio for me when I arrived at our family home. She hugged me. I was about to discover things about my life as a little child I couldn't remember or hadn't ever known had happened. As Mum unfolded to me what had happened those many years before, I was deeply shocked.

She described how we had outgrown the flat where I had been born. My parents had bought a new home in a suburb nearby after the birth of their fourth child. We had moved into our new home. Three days later, my sister and I were playing in the children's sandpit at the bottom of the enormous garden which was like a child's paradise to us after having lived in a flat. Now, we could enjoy the freedom of being able to run and play freely outside in the fresh air and sunshine.

I was three and a half years old at the time, a small child with dark hair and pale green eyes. On that fateful day, my older sister and I were playing and laughing and having great fun. Mum called her to the house, and I was left to enjoy our new-found play area on my own.

A short little man with dark beady eyes appeared at the boundary wall and called to me, "Little girl, come with me. I have sweets and silver paper for you." The school children in those days collected silver paper, mostly chocolate wrappers, to raise funds for various charities. My sister had been collecting silver paper for her school charity and so I thought she would be so happy with me if I got some for her. Younger siblings always try to please the older ones. I was no different.

The little man lifted me over the wall and took me into the house next door. I remember little except that the house was very dark inside and I remember the sound of a door being locked. Apparently, my mother and sister were calling for me so the man unlocked the door and let me go. Mum said that, when I got home, I told her where I had been and what had happened. "That man tried to wee-wee in my pants and he hurt me, Mommy," I said.

Mum was horrified. Grabbing all four of her children, Mum rushed to the nearby building site where my father was working. She told me how Dad went absolutely crazy and wanted '. . . to kill that man!' Fortunately, she persuaded him to go to the police station and allow the law to deal with him.

This perverted man was living with his sister in the house next door to our new home and I was the fourth child under the age of five that he had molested in four years. My parents were appalled as they with their three daughters were living next door to this monster. He had committed the same crime three times and each time had been released into his sister's custody as he was supposedly 'not right in his head'. He had definitely slipped through the legal system.

In those days, Child Welfare didn't protect children as it does today. At three and a half years of age, I had to personally appear in court and tell the court what this man had done to me.

When my father saw how I was being cross-questioned by the attorneys in the courtroom, he demanded they stop. The judge called for a recess so that he might speak to Dad. He explained that if I didn't testify, the case would be dismissed and once again the accused man would go free. The judge reiterated how serious the situation had now become. A conviction had to be secured as this was fourth offence. Each of the previous cases had been dismissed because the parents of the other children wouldn't allow them to testify. Having heard this, Dad allowed the attorneys continue on condition that they didn't raise their voices to me and stood a certain distance from me when questioning me. I was allowed to testify to ensure my abuser would never be able to perpetrate a similar crime on any child again.

I had been too young to remember any of this. What little I could remember I had blocked out of my mind . . . that is, until the attempted robbery in the garage some 24 years later.

Mum and I were weeping as she continued to sketch in the details of this horrible incident. My abuser was sentenced to spend the rest of his natural life in a mental institution.

Now, for the first time, all those dreams and images which had plagued me made complete sense to me. I had recently become a committed Christian and knew I had to forgive the man. He was mentally ill. How could I hold that against him?

I was, however, very disturbed about the other monster, who was still alive. I later found out that he also had full knowledge of all the details of my dreadful ordeal as a three and a half year old child. I now realised why he had kept telling me that I had done something bad. Knowing all this, he still continued to abuse me and make my life a deep misery until I was almost 12 years old. Unlike the horrible ordeal I had experienced as a very little girl, this on-going trauma I could clearly remember in great detail.

After Mum's harrowing account of my first molestation, she pleaded with me to tell her who the other man was. I couldn't. I was overwhelmed by a feeling that it would cause far too much trouble and pain to so many innocent people. I felt I couldn't summon the courage or strength to deal with something which would inevitably involve others, who had had nothing to do with the awful events. As it was I was dealing with my own personal confusion and pain at this time. Mum didn't pursue the matter. She understood me so well and promised she would be there for me when I was ready to talk about it.

Many people have asked me since that time of revelation, "Why didn't you tell your parents what this man was doing to you all those years?" Until someone experiences abuse, they cannot begin to understand how one becomes trapped into silence. I had been so scared of my molester who constantly threatened me. The tactics he used to control me were very powerful. I blamed myself for what was happening and believed the abuse was punishment for my being bad when I was younger. My abuser kept drumming into me that I had always been a very bad girl. I was consumed with anxiety about getting myself into trouble if I said anything. The worst part of molestation is the shame and there no words to describe what havoc this shame wreaks on the victims of molestation. All of this was true of me as I became locked into a prison of silence.

As I wrestled with the flood of memories stirred up by what Mum had told me and my sharing the painful memories of the on-going time of molestation, I found myself justifying why I couldn't and shouldn't ever forgive my second abuser. I nearly drove myself crazy, turning these thoughts over and over in my mind. I found myself consumed with hatred for him and wished he were dead. Then, I would be horrified that I could have such awful thoughts about another human being. Vernon was still away on business during those days of mental turmoil. God was so gracious in removing my husband from the situation, so that that He may help me to be whole again in His way and time. I only had Him to turn to. It was God and me alone. Something totally unexpected was about to happen.

I went home extremely disturbed and emotionally drained after my visits to Mum and the doctor. What I had found out about myself over the last 24 hours had really shocked me. That afternoon, I asked God to help me sort out this awful, deeply disturbing situation in which I found myself. I really didn't know where to begin. I needed a miracle of His forgiveness, love, peace and wisdom.

While I was resting that same afternoon, my mind was filled with the image of the man who had violated my innocence being locked in a cage and my being shut in another. I became aware of a third figure holding a bunch of keys in His hand and pacing between the two cages. Somehow, I knew immediately it was God! At first I was puzzled, but then I understood what I was seeing. We were both prisoners. God could not heal me or begin to work in the man's life while we were both imprisoned in the cages. I had to choose to forgive him. As I did, God would first unlock my cage. Then He would hand me the keys and I would set this man free. I had to make the choice to forgive. As I forgave the man who had abused me for so long, God would forgive him. We would both be released from our prisons. I struggled against doing this. I felt so intensely that he did not deserve my forgiveness for wha he had done. Only when someone has been so wounded as I had been, can they understand how impossible it is to truly forgive. I may have accepted an apology. I may have said that I forgave him. I certainly would never again have had anything to do with him. I believe what I felt at that time was a natural form of self-preservation to avoid ever being hurt again.

That night, before going to sleep, I prayed fervently for God to help me. My head was telling me to forgive him . . . it was the right thing to do. I was experiencing such agony in my heart as I tussled with my conflicting emotions. I couldn't summon the willpower to say those three words . . . "I forgive you". I begged the Lord for help. In my mind, I had a vivid picture of Jesus hanging on the cross, gazing down at the people below Him. I remembered his words so clearly from my years of reading them in the Bible: "Father, forgive them for they know not what they do." My whole being was flooded with the healing inherent in those words. For the first time since the awful experience, I knew this man had never known or understood the extent of the pain and damage he had inflicted on me. Surely no human being could be so cruel intentionally?

I battled with the thought that, strange as it may seem, this man, who had behaved in such a monstrous way towards me, was a nice person in so many other ways . . . such a likeable and very ordinary family man.

"Oh Lord, my mind tells me I must forgive him, but my heart says I can't and I shouldn't," I prayed. "Please give me your forgiveness for him. I don't want to hate him or hold this terrible crime against him, but I don't know how to do this". I pleaded with the Lord, "Take out my hard, unforgiving heart. Give me a heart filled with your love and forgiveness."

I sobbed myself to sleep. When I awoke in the small hours of the morning, I knew immediately God had answered me. The ugliness I had felt towards the man was no longer there. The ache in the pit of my stomach that I had felt for as long as I could remember, had also gone. That awful anger and hatred was gone! They had been replaced by such a peace and a desire to forgive him. I wept and wept. I experienced the years of hurt, brokenness and pain being washed away by my tears. The deep crying lasted for what seemed like ages. That night, God unlocked my cage. He gave me the keys so that I could now unlock the cage in which my violator had been imprisoned. I felt a deep sadness for his wife and family . . . such good, wonderful people whom I loved very much. A great compassion for him and his family flooded me. It was hard to understand my change of heart . . . it was like night and day. I felt such a sense of relief that I had never revealed his name to anyone.

The next time I saw him, the peace I felt in my heart gave me such assurance that my forgiveness of him had been real and complete. It is said that the mirror of the soul is in the eyes. All those years, I had never been able to look into the man's eyes. When we met that day, I walked up to him, looked him straight in the eyes and greeted him as I would have anyone else I knew. I saw such emptiness and sadness. I felt such compassion for him and silently asked God to reveal Himself to this pitiable man. I had a deep conviction that he too had an aching need to find a relationship with God. He needed the same forgiveness and healing I had been so blessed to have received.

At every function from then on at which we were both present, he would come to sit and talk with me. Shortly after that significant meeting, we were both at a wedding. That day, I had the privilege of being able to share my personal relationship with God with him. It flowed so easily and he was so receptive. He hung on my every word as I shared my faith and the love of Christ with him. I never discussed the abuse of all those years ago. As I spoke to him, I saw a peace come into the eyes of my former tormentor. I felt so blessed to have been able to play a significant part in his restoration.

By the time Vernon returned from his trip, God had completed a wonderful work in me. I was able to share with my husband all that had happened while he had been away. At first he was shocked and very upset. He couldn't understand why I had never told him all this before. As we talked, he realised that I had never even known or understood most of it myself. It was only when my mother had told me the whole story and my doctor had explained the complexities of the human brain, that I realised I had put up a block in my mind about the second man who had abused me as a child. This barrier was torn down during the attempted robbery. We talked and cried together well into the early hours of the morning. Vernon was so happy that he now understood why I had been such a fearful person all through our married life.

My silence had allowed the abuse to continue and it had kept my pain alive. It had protected my abuser and prolonged my suffering as it enabled him to carry on molesting me. I am so thankful I was able to break my silence. The benefits of sharing the story of my being abused with safe people were innumerable. It was only when I took that first step of talking to my doctor, that healing was possible and the journey to eventual total restoration begun. I had lived in denial, had hidden the awful truth and had buried it for 24years. I had to bring it into the light in order for something positive to be done about it for both myself and our marriage.

I had loved being married and had wanted us to have children, however, if I have to be honest, the intimacy aspect of marriage was a duty I endured. The years of molestation were to blame. Deep down, Vernon had realised there was something amiss, but he was so gentle and kind over the first eight years of our marriage. Looking back, I realised how wonderfully tolerant he was of me with all my fears. Now we were both so excited, looking forward to the changes that were now possible in our life together. After my healing, we enjoyed many wonderful years of normal married life until he got ill and died shortly after our 35th wedding anniversary.

Many years later, the same family friend who had abused me became ill. His wife cared for him herself. As his sole carer, she was often in a terrible emotional state as his illness was very difficult for her to cope with. She was devoted to him. During that time, I would help her, looking after him while she went shopping, to church or visited her children or friends. She desperately needed some respite. I would spend those times taking him for walks, reading to him or talking with him. We spent many happy, peaceful hours together during those 18 months before his death. I was so glad I had not erected the wall of self-preservation around myself, which so often happens when people are trying to cope with hurt and trauma. I was enabled to be a vehicle of blessing to this needy couple. God never ceases to amaze me with the way in which He acts to make ways through seemingly impossible situations.

I can honestly say I could never have done it in my own strength and without God's help! With His help, it was not difficult at all. I was stunned. God had helped me and He will help anyone who asks. He has no favourites. He loves us all the same.

So often, I had heard the saying, "Forgive and forget." For years, I had been so puzzled by this. How can one possibly forget such an awful memory as the one which plagued me? It is impossible to wipe out a memory . . . it doesn't simply evaporate.

Today, I understand what that maxim means: the memory remains; it can't be erased but God heals the pain attached to the memory. It's the pain that one forgets. The proof that I have both forgiven and forgotten is that I am able to share this so freely with people. I bear no grudge towards either of these men. I feel no pain, only joy that his family were spared the knowledge and the pain of what I had endured.

Shortly after my original visit to him, my doctor contacted me. He was anxious that I receive counselling with a psychologist. I was able to share with him that I didn't need to see one as I was absolutely fine. He was not convinced and said I should contact him at any time if I felt the need to talk again or if I wanted to go for counselling at a later date. I have never needed to go back to him or a psychologist. God did a 'complete' work in me for which I am so grateful. This was a great testimony to both my doctor and my parents, through whom so much of God's healing came.

Three years before Mum died, I went to look after her while she was recovering from surgery. One night, she couldn't sleep and so we were having a cup of tea and chatting at three in the morning. While we were talking, she brought up the subject of my abuse for the first time since I'd been emotionally healed. I was now in my late fifties. Mum told me that during her illness, she had been thinking a great deal about my ordeal, something she hadn't done in a long while. She said she suspected a certain person and asked me if her hunch was right. It was. For the first time in my life, I was able to acknowledge who he was to someone else. She said it had saddened her greatly that I had never come to her while the molestation was happening. She would have protected me and stopped it. Nonetheless, she understood how fearful my abuser had made me. We cried together again that night. Mum said it grieved her that I had paid such a high price to protect his family from being hurt. It hurt her deeply that I had forfeited a normal carefree childhood.

I believe the way God allowed my particular case to be dealt with was indeed the best way for me. The result was that his family were spared the shame and pain. Looking back, I can honestly say I cannot see what purpose it would have served for me to take legal action against him at that late stage of my life. I don't believe I could have coped with any more emotional trauma at that particular time. This was definitely a case of contrary rather than the rule.

Now, however, I do think differently. I believe the only route should be criminal charges being laid against the offender to ensure he is not able to continue abusing other victims. I believe in my heart that I probably was an isolated victim of this particular man. I say this because, at the first opportunity, I tactfully asked my sisters and a few family friends if anyone had ever interfered with them sexually. I found I was able to broach the subject quite easily to them once Mum had told me about the incident which had happened when I was three and a half. I never mentioned the other man, and they all replied that nobody had ever tried to do anything to them. If there were others, I will never know.

Most of the victims of abuse I have spoken to want two things from their abuser. Firstly, they want an apology without rationalisations and justifications. Then they need a guarantee that the same thing will never happen to anyone else. I want to say from the outset that neither of those may ever happen. In my case, I never had either. God helped me in a totally different way.

Do I believe my heartache and pain was wasted? Definitely not! I do believe God redeemed my situation and brought much good out of it. I trusted Him and was prepared to forgive. In the end, I was the greatest beneficiary.

The question may be asked, "What good could possibly come out of something so awful?" I'm now in my sixties and have had the privilege of sharing my overcoming experience with different groups of women and privately with those who have heard of my experience and have been referred to me by family or friends. My address is not an academic topic . . . I've lived it.

It's been so sad to see so many women trapped in silence, as I had been, after they had endured similar experiences. Of those I have personally dealt with, 95% of the women have been abused by family members or close family friends—the very ones who should have been protecting them. So many of those I have personally met and spoken with have gained new hope and courage and ultimately found 'there is life after abuse'. The truth sets you free.

I now see a beautiful picture of God's Grace . . . through my pain and brokenness. He crafted me into a tool He could use to bring hope and healing to others. I survived and so can those who have suffered like me!

MARRIAGE SHOULD BE
100/100 NOT 50/50

When I got married in 1969, I was so ignorant about what a real marriage relationship ought to be. Experience, it seemed to me then, was definitely the teacher in many marriages. Since coming into a relationship with God, I have discovered that the Bible is the only trustworthy book that lays down clear foundations and guidelines in all areas of life, and certainly in marriage, and which work every time. The individual needs to search for that guidance themselves and then choose to put it into practice. When I first got married, I was carried away by the romance, the feeling of being loved by someone, the excitement of a wedding, the physical attraction, and perhaps by having a husband to meet some of my needs and inadequacies. That was what I called "marriage".

Having been born into a large family where every member had very strong personalities, I was determined that no man was going to dominate and control me when I married him. I lived married life "my way" for eight years before discovering these practical Biblical principles. I decided to apply them to both my personal and my married life.

Before this "revelation", my maternal grandparents' and my own parents' marriages had been my only examples. They influenced me to a certain extent, but it was my new-found Biblical perspective which taught me the difference between a submissive wife and a 'doormat'. Sadly, too many men have a very distorted understanding of what submission in their wives really means. I started my marriage by being a domineering and controlling wife. Thank God He helped not to stay that way! After living these Biblical principles over the years, I came to realise that a good, loving, responsible marriage is not one where 50/50 is the order of the day. Each partner is called to give100% to the other!

My maternal grandparents, fondly known to us as "Papa" and "Mama", were married for 62 years. As their granddaughter, I admired the reverence, respect, honour and devotion showed by Mama to my grandfather. I adored them both when I was a child. They were everything perfect grandparents could ever be. During my childhood, I never heard a raised voice or witnessed an argument between them. I thought they had a perfect marriage.

They had had five children and lived at that time on a sugar estate in Mauritius, where my grandfather was a business man who also owned and trained racehorses. Mama was an excellent seamstress and a devoted wife, mother and homemaker. Both of my grand-parents' mothers were widowed at an early age. In those days, widowed parents usually went to live with one of their children. Both grandmothers lived in the same home with Papa, Mama and their children. They all firmly believed this was an excellent recipe for a successful marriage and family life. The extended family was a vital aspect of their family's life. It not only helped with the running of the home, but also with the raising of the children. Mama said, "Papa and I were always on our best behaviour and polite to one another in front of our mothers. Although we did have our disagreements in private, we respected and honoured them too much to ever upset them".

Marriage was not always so blissful for them, as I found out later on in life when Mama began to share some of her experiences with me. I had been married a few years when I paid her a visit. I discovered for the first time some of the difficulties she had encountered being married to a handsome, charming Frenchman. Soon after Papa's death, I went to visit Mama who was then living alone in an apartment. I'd had an argument with Vernon that day and decided I would visit Mama to 'cool off'. I hadn't mentioned a word about our argument, when, out of the blue, she said to me, "Angela, marriage is not always easy, my darling. It is hard work and you have to work at it your whole life." It seemed as though she knew exactly what I thinking and feeling.

She went on to tell me her story. "Because you are married now, my girl, Mama can tell you these things" she said in her broken English. This was the first time my grandmother had ever spoken to me about 'private' matters. Private matters like these were never discussed with unmarried women.

I will never forget my shock and horror the first time she divulged her story to me. My problems seemed so petty compared to what this gracious lady had endured almost all her married life. Whenever I felt a bit low or things were difficult in my marriage, my best counsellor was my precious Mama.

She told me how, during the early years of her marriage whilst they were still living in Mauritius, most men of that time had mistresses. Papa was no exception. She told me of when she had first stumbled on this sad truth and of how she handled it. I can still hear her words in her broad French accent. She told him, "France, I will remain your wife until the day I die. I have had five children with you and I will always be your wife and mother of your children in this home. I will never leave you. No matter how many women you have in your life, I will stay . . . and no divorce!" She told me of the many times she had to entertain his "lady friends" at her dining table. I was horrified—how could she have managed it? This was where the two grandmothers proved invaluable to her. Grand Mere Jan, Papa's mother, was blatantly rude to these women. Grand Mere de Baize, Mama's mother, remained the perfect lady, casting icy glares of disapproval at the poor woman of the moment throughout the meal. Mama said she actually felt sorry for these women when they came face to face with the two formidable grandmothers around the dinner table. Both grandmothers also made it very clear to Papa that no woman other than Mama would ever be accepted by them. When they moved to South Africa the two grandmothers chose to remain in Mauritius and end their days there.

Papa and Mama often visited their mothers and siblings in Mauritius regularly but made a new life for themselves in South Africa.

"Oh Angela, it got easier with each new lady friend. I knew they wouldn't last. Sooner or later, when they found out I would never give him a divorce, they disappeared. I remained calm, determined and always 'a lady', and I won in the end." Even when they came to live in South Africa in 1944, Papa's good looks, accent and charm always assured him of much attention from the ladies. The last time he was unfaithful to her was when she was 65years old. Papa asked her to move out of the marital home as he wanted his lady friend to move in with him. For the first time in all their marriage Mama agreed to accommodate his unfaithfulness, much to the shock of her children who adored her. She got an apartment and furnished it with the best furnishings. Strange as it may seem, she never spent a single night in that apartment. The first week she spent with one daughter and the second with another. After two weeks, Papa turned up at our home where Mama was staying at the time. With cap in hand, he pleaded with my mother to ask Mama to come back home. He wept confessing he had made the biggest mistake of his life and promised he would never look at another woman again. My mother was furious and said, "Papa, you asked Mama to leave you. Now, you ask her to come back!" That cured him completely of his philandering. Until his death, he remained devoted to her and couldn't put her on a higher pedestal or do enough for her.

I asked Mama why she tolerated this lifestyle . . . she was beautiful, efficient and the perfect wife and mother. Her reply was always the same, "My darling, I married him for better or worse, and my better days were far more than my worse days. I stayed because I had made a vow before God. I loved him, and he was a good husband and father, even if you can't understand that. I am so glad I stood my ground and we ended our days together".

With my own parents' marriage, I saw my mother as the proverbial 'doormat'. Dad was extremely controlling, demanding and possessive of Mum, yet she was always gracious, answering his every beck and call. Even though Dad has gone to be with the Lord, I have no intention of 'canonising' him as a saint as many people do after losing someone close to them. I was often on the receiving end of his abruptness and many times I would tell him, "Dad, I love you but I certainly don't like you sometimes." Having said that, I will always say in his defence that, even though he was difficult (and he knew he was), he was never too proud to admit it. He would apologise and make restitution when he'd overstepped the mark. I found this an honourable trait in his character. I have no doubt whatsoever that they loved one another deeply, but my father was very difficult at times. Because Dad had grown up in a dysfunctional family as I mentioned earlier, he had no example of what a normal married life should be. Being a politician only exacerbated the situation. He had developed a tough shell around himself to cope with the harsh realities that come with that particular occupation. Mother always blamed his upbringing and his being a public figure as the reasons for his bad attitude at times. She was probably right to a certain extent, but I felt she should not have made excuses for him. He was now an adult and should have been able to take full responsibility for himself. Later on in their marriage, however, she did begin to stand up for herself. She certainly got Father's attention on those rare occasions! Sadly, it was only much later in life that he mellowed and changed. For all that, he was a faithful husband, a good father, a hard worker and wonderful provider for his very large family.

I have to admit I did learn some lessons from both the good and bad experiences of my parents' and grandparents' marriages.

My own marriage didn't get off to a great start. I came into it burdened with the baggage of my molestation. This was only dealt with 8 years into our marriage when my relationship with God developed. My strict Catholic upbringing had laid a solid foundation of faithfulness, discipline and many other good attributes in my life. For that, I will always be grateful. However, I had never had a personal relationship with Jesus Christ. During my many years of attending church, I had known 'about' Him but never 'known' Him.

When I met Vernon, he too was a Catholic but had never attended Church regularly. We were married in the Catholic Church and went through a strict pre—marriage counselling course. It was compulsory for all couples contemplating marriage in the Church to attend

Mass regularly and complete this course. I learned much from those counselling sessions, but on their own, they weren't the complete answer. We needed so much more than that for a good marriage.

When I came into my own relationship with God, He healed me emotionally from the aftermath of my molestation as a child and in many other areas which had hampered my growth as an emotionally, mentally and spiritually healthy person. Those effects of that healing gradually filtered through to every part of my life, including my marriage. I cannot say it was easy . . . it wasn't. There were still many issues within myself that I had to deal with if I wanted my marriage to succeed.

Vernon and I were invited to a Marriage Encounter course. He shocked me by agreeing to go. The course entailed a weekend away with about twenty other couples. After the introductory talk, he told me he felt we didn't need this. If he still felt the same in the morning, we would be going home. I felt we desperately did need it but kept silent. I asked God to have His way and speak to Vernon. It never ceases to amaze me how many men firmly believe their marriage is fine and that they don't need any outside help to make it better. On the other hand, most women are open to almost anything that will help them improve their marriages. I firmly believe this to be an 'ego thing' with men. Vernon never mentioned going home again and we had a very blessed, wonderful weekend. He received so much from the Marriage Encounter course. After many years of not attending church, he decided to come with me every Sunday. He was invited by the course leaders to share his experience of our Encounter weekend the following Sunday morning at Mass. Many couples were touched by what he shared.

Soon after coming into my relationship with God, I realised I had many changes to make within myself. I had heard the injunction, 'wives be submissive to your husbands' all my life. I loathed hearing it. To me, the word 'submission' was like a red rag to a bull and brought out the very worst in me. I realised later on, when I had a proper understanding of the word 'submission', how stubborn and ignorant I had been for so long . . . how I had wasted so much precious time. 'Submission' in relation to marriage is one of the most misused and abused words. In my ignorance, my interpretation of it was to 'be a doormat'. I had seen the 'doormat' scenario in both my mother and grandmother's marriages. I vowed I would never allow that to happen to me! Sadly, for quite a while, as I was dealing with my rebellion, pride and ignorance, Vernon and I forfeited several years which could have been so much happier and easier for both of us had I dealt with this issue earlier.

Fear was something else that hindered me from submitting to my husband sooner. I feared that if I became submissive, I would become too vulnerable and Vernon would take advantage of that.

I feel so strongly about sharing what true submission in a marriage is. I believe there are many women who believe mistakenly as I believed. God clearly formulated the job descriptions in marriage for both husband and wife. Ephesians 5:25 describes the duties of a godly husband: "Husbands, love your wives just as Christ loved the Church and gave Himself for her." The godly wife's job description is found in Ephesians 5:22: "Wives, submit to your own husband as to the Lord." By submitting my life to God first, I was enabled to submit to my husband. A simple definition of submission is treating your spouse with reverence, honour and respect. I could, with confidence, submit decisions, plans and ideas concerning both myself and the family to Vernon, and trust and believe that God would guide him, as the head of our family, to make the right decisions. If we ever had differing opinions, ideas or tastes (which happened often), as a submissive wife, I could openly share my feelings with him. He would know what my ideas or opinions were. I would quietly ask God to show him, 'as the head of our home', the wise and correct solution for our marriage and family. Before this, I had thought my job description was to 'straighten him out'. He had had to endure my getting angry, insisting on my own way, and totally ignoring his ideas and wishes. I would shout him down and 'just go ahead' and do what I thought was right, whether he liked it or not. That was how I had lived in the past. Now, I had to quit it, admit it, forget it. I needed to move on to be the woman God had called me to be. I am truly ashamed of my behaviour during those first few years of our marriage.

Submission humbled me in a way nothing else could have and I needed a huge dose of it!

Some practical instances speak clearly of how we experienced living 100/100 for each other. We discovered this to be the only way of bringing true happiness, peace and fulfilment to our marriage.

One day, Vernon came home from work and told me the company had offered him an insurance policy to cover his salary for 6 months in the case of illness or an accident. We had three young children and were struggling financially, so I immediately responded, "Vernon, we can't afford it! Anyway, you have never been off sick even for one day. We definitely will not be able to take it".

Shortly after that conversation, I went to bath. The bathroom seemed to be the place where God often dealt with me. It was the only really quiet place I was able to be alone and away from the hustle and bustle of family life. As I relaxed in the bath, my thoughts wandered back to the conversation I had just had with Vernon. I began questioning myself: "You were very rude and abrupt to Vernon. Is he really the head of our home? You never even asked his opinion. That conversation was one-sided. What if something serious did happen?"

This marked the turning point in my attitude to submission and change in my behaviour. What a wakeup call I had in the bathroom that evening! I had asked God to help me be the best wife and mother only a week before. He was wasting no time at all! I told the Lord I was sorry for reacting the way I had and asked Him to help me be a godly wife. After a short while, I came out of the bathroom a very different person to the one who had gone in. I went into the living room and hugged Vernon, apologising for my outburst. He smiled, hugged me back and told me not to worry. I asked him to explain the policy to me, which he did. I assured him that the decision was his. He must do what he felt was best for the family as I trusted his judgement. He smiled again, saying, "Okay, I'll give it some thought. I will make a decision by the end of the week". Strangely enough, I never asked him at the end of the week what he had decided, and he didn't tell me. Six months later I found out what he had done.

Vernon had offered to help a friend of mine to do some alterations at her nursery school. She was in a difficult financial position, so she purchased the materials and he supplied his labour free of charge, doing the work over his weekends. One Saturday morning, when the job was nearly completed, my friend and I were in the local mall with our children while Vernon was working on the roof at the school. One of the maids from the school came running into the mall, screaming to us to come quickly. Vernon had fallen off the roof and was badly hurt.

Since early that morning, I had had a feeling of uneasiness in the pit of my stomach. I felt something was amiss but could not put my finger on it. When I heard the maid screaming, this heaviness lifted and a peace flooded my whole being. I couldn't understand it. Normally I would have panicked. I asked Cathy to go on to the Nursery School and get help as soon as possible. I needed to leave the children with my mother. I really didn't want them to see their father injured.

I wasn't prepared to find Vernon so badly hurt. He was sprawled on the ground. Both his legs were broken and his one foot and ankle were so badly broken that the bones were protruding through the skin. A neighbour had already called an ambulance. I knelt beside him, cradled his head and asked, "Why? Why?" He was only being kind, helping someone in need . . . and now this dreadful accident had happened!

Suddenly Vernon opened his eyes and said, "No, Angela! You mustn't ask 'why'." It shocked me to hear him speak like that. Only a few weeks before, I had received the blessing of the gift of praying in the Spirit (speaking in tongues) after having opposed it vehemently for many years. I immediately said, "I'm sorry, Lord. I don't understand this but I'm going to trust you." I then started to pray in the Spirit.

During the ambulance ride to the hospital, I held Vernon's hand and continued praying. Suddenly he opened his eye. I stopped praying. H said, "I don't know what you're saying but don't stop." He had never heard me pray in the Spirit. Later, he told me he had somehow known it was right as he felt so peaceful. He opened his eyes again and said, "Angie, you won't have to worry about my salary. I took out that insurance." I couldn't believe my ears! My first concern was to get him to the hospital as he was so badly injured. My second concern would surely have been how would we survive? I wasn't working at that time and his was the only income coming into our home.

When someone prays in their heavenly language, the Holy Spirit knows your needs before they even occur. God knew we would have to survive for almost five months without a salary. Vernon would not be able to work due to his injury but God had supplied our need. My husband was seriously injured and had sustained permanent disability in his left foot. He limped for the rest of his life. He had used his headship in the home for the right purpose, because I had 'let' him. This was just one example of how the change in me allowed God to bless our marriage. Day after day, God taught me through everyday situations in our lives how to live 100% for each other.

Vernon spent four months in a wheelchair and seven months on crutches. It was a challenging time for the whole family but God used the situation to 'break me, melt me, and mould me' into the wife He had called me to be. As I chose to meet Vernon's every need with the right attitude of heart, love, respect and honour, he, in turn, committed his life to Christ. He began complimenting me and telling me how blessed and happy he felt in every area of his life, but most especially in our marriage.

Another example that stands out in my mind occurred about a year later. One day, Vernon phoned me from work and asked what we were having for dinner. I told him I was cooking sausage, mash and onion gravy. I stopped and said, "We were going to have that. Would you like something else?" "Yes", he answered. "Do you think I could have my favourite?" I knew what it was . . . steak, egg and chips. "No problem," I answered.

The children were 'on top form' that afternoon, arguing, messing and generally being difficult. I started preparing the supper and thought, "I hope Vernon comes home on time". I was exhausted and had intended leaving his food in the warmer. The type of meal he wanted needed to be prepared and eaten straight away. It was definitely not a put-in-the-warmer type; There and then I made the decision to give 100%.

I finished my chores, fed and settled the children in their beds. It just so happened that Vernon was much later than normal on that particular day. He rang again to say he was stuck in a traffic jam. He sounded exhausted and told me he had had really had a difficult day at work. He said he would be home in about an hour and a half. I set the table before having a quick bath. I was thankful that everything was going to be perfect for his homecoming.

I felt really good that I had done the right thing and was refreshed and looked forward to my husband coming home. I dressed casually, sprayed on my perfume and started cooking our dinner. I was just putting the finishing touches to the meal when Vernon walked through the front door. "Wow! This is like walking into Heaven! How do you do it?" he asked. "While I was stuck in the traffic, I thought to myself that I hoped I could relax when I get home. I am so tired but my homecoming couldn't have been better, I am the luckiest man in the World!" After dinner, he put down his knife and fork and told me that it had been one of the best meals I had ever made. How different it might have been if I had done what 'I had felt' like doing just because I was too tired.

The 'old' me would have thought, "They're his children. He should realise what I go through 24/7 every day. Let him have a taste of it and deal with them when he gets home. Then he will appreciate me more". Oh no, he wouldn't have! I know that now. He loved coming home. Home was his haven . . . a place where he could be refreshed and relax in peace and quiet; a place where he could enjoy have fun times with the children, playing board games, swimming in the pool and just talking over the dinner table. Submitting to my husband made him so happy and, at the same time, ensured my happiness. As he was happy, he wanted to make me happy at every opportunity he got. When we first married, neither of us knew that, during our years together, we would encounter some very difficult and painful situations. We experienced circumstances which we could have easily used to justify separation or even divorce. Because of our deep commitment to each other, we worked through those situations. I am so glad we did.

In a society as uncommitted as today's, many people go through multiple relationships, almost always vainly hoping, after each split-up, that they will meet Mr or Ms Right and that this new relationship will be 'The One'. Sadly, so often, a few months down the line, they will have parted ways. It never fails to amaze me how many celebrities and hosts on talk-shows, who have never been married, tell their gullible audiences (and our children) that, "The times have changed. We must move with them. It's not the same today as in our parents days. Marriage is just a piece of paper." . . . words used to justify their lack of willingness to commit themselves to another person. They flaunt their selfish lifestyles as "the modern way of doing things."

When the going got tough and problems and illness came our way, we were so grateful for having a deeply committed relationship that held us together and carried us through many difficult times. A happy home, a good marriage and a loving family life are endangered species today and are in desperate need of protection and nurturing. Men generally find it hard to express their negative innermost feelings, fears and thoughts. Vernon was no exception, but we eventually came to a place in our relationship where neither of us was afraid to be vulnerable with the other.

God challenged me to become a submissive wife and, with that challenge, He equipped me with the revelation and knowledge of how and the ability to be the woman He had called me to be in marriage. My patience and kindness were tested for quite a while before Vernon changed. There was no reason why I should have been surprised at that . . . I'd been a very different person for years before I had decided to change. As I began respecting, honouring and loving Vernon unconditionally, he started to realise this was a lasting change in me. His heart began to soften and he too was drawn to the Christ who lived in me. Thank God I chose to change and can strongly recommend that living 100/100 for each other was the best thing that could have happened to our marriage.

Chapter 4 ────────────────────────

LOSING RELIGION AND GAINING
A RELATIONSHIP WITH GOD

From the time I was a very little girl, my Mum taught me about God. She was a Catholic and attended Church regularly. Dad, on the other hand, claimed to belong to the Church of England and the only times he darkened the doors of a church were on rare special occasions. When I was about seven years old, Dad's Uncle Clifford came to visit him in South Africa. He encouraged Dad to join the Free Masons, which he did. Mum was furious. He attended their meetings for a few years and then suddenly stopped going to the lodge. From a fun loving, affectionate Dad he became withdrawn and cold. We were never told why he left except that he had encountered something that had disturbed him terribly. Later on when I was older I asked Mum why he had left and she said she couldn't tell me and she asked me not to ever bring the subject up as it had upset Dad so much. So I never did.

Mum, by contrast, was devout in her faith. She made sure we were all christened, made our First Holy Communion and were confirmed at the appropriate times. We were all sent to private convent schools as were all good Catholics in those days. I conformed in every way. Following my Mum's example, I regularly went to Mass and did everything expected of a practising Catholic.

As I grew older, I began questioning certain aspects of my religion. I found there were Catholic teachings for which I believed there was no scriptural basis. When I asked questions, I was told, "Angela, it's not for us to question. Why are you always questioning everything about our faith? Our ancestors were all Catholics and we believe it to be the one true faith." Being a naturally inquisitive child and not easily deterred, I delved into history books and encyclopaedias looking for answers. I came to the point where I felt strongly that, unless I could see a direct scriptural basis for a doctrine, I must reject it. I became totally disillusioned as I discovered more and more areas where I believed this biblical undergirding was lacking. I found what I saw as man-made traditions, rules and regulations.

Thankfully, many of these antiquated traditions have now been abandoned. Sadly, many of the questions which had bothered me remained unanswered until I was about twenty six years. It was then that a good friend of mine committed suicide. I was devastated.

This dear friend too had been molested as a young boy in the local park. Because his father, an immigrant to South Africa, was an extremely strict man, my friend was never able to tell him about it. So often, I had seen his father treat him very cruelly in ways which today would definitely be considered child abuse. He told his mother about the incident when it happened, but she too was afraid of her husband's bad temper and told her son to never mention "that nonsense" to her or anyone else ever again. So, like me, he too had to keep his dark secret to himself. That was, until we made friends and he felt free to tell me all about it. I was too ashamed to tell him I was still being molested when I met him. All I said was that I had also been molested in the past. I suppose because we shared the same problem, we found solace in each other. We understood one another and felt safe discussing our lives with each other. He was always very protective and kind to me. We felt very comfortable with each other. It was like a brother/sister relationship.

My friend went overseas for a while in his early twenties and, during that time, I met my future husband. By the time he returned, I was engaged to be married. I left Durban and lost contact with him for a long while.

Years later, I got a phone call telling me of his tragic untimely demise. He had taken his own life. His death caused me to really seek answers and to search for this God that everyone else but me seemed to know. I was discussing this tragedy with a very attentive elderly family friend. She offered to help me find the answers I had been seeking for so long. She attended the local Spiritualist Church and invited me to go along with her. My mother was horrified. I was now an adult . . . she could not prevent me from going. With hindsight, I wish I had been more attentive to my mother's warnings.

I attended a few Spiritualist meetings. I was riveted when the medium came up with the facts which seemed to fit my situation exactly. She said to me, "The other pea in the pod turns twenty one soon and she's blonde, blue eyed and very happy." I had lost a sister who was a twin at birth. I was rocked by this revelation because my younger brother, my late sister's twin, was about to celebrate his twenty first birthday two weeks later. Just as his sister had been, he was fair and blue eyed.

The medium also mentioned the initials E.V . . . . the initials of my childhood friend that had recently committed suicide. These communications from "the other side" shocked me. I was curious to know how she knew about these very private issues in my life. I wondered if the family friend had given her this information. I realised she didn't know about my sister and she certainly didn't know my friend's name.

Only much later did I realise that, although what this spiritualist said to me was true, it didn't necessarily make it right. From the time I started going to these séances, I soon became dependent on tranquilizers. I became a nervous wreck. I had always thought that spiritual experiences were supposed to make you feel calm and peaceful. I had never been more disturbed in my entire life. I had gone there for answers but only came away with more unanswered questions. I visited my local parish Priest and various people from my congregation, trying to find answers to my many questions and explanations of all these disturbing things which were happening to me. All they were able to tell me was that it was wrong and evil. They couldn't substantiate what they told me.

Eventually, I came across someone who gave me books to read and the common sense answers I had been seeking for so long. She was a committed Christian. I had always admired her gentle spirit and loved her peaceful countenance. I felt I could trust her wise, humble and caring counsel. She had a practical answer for every question I put to her and all her answers made so much sense to me.

Because of God's Word and the advice this wise Christian lady had given me, I came to the conviction that Spiritualism was not for me. After a whole year, I stopped attending the spiritualist services. But the damage was done. I was on the verge of a nervous breakdown and I still had no closure to the loss of my friend.

At this same time, the hospital that had prescribed tranquilisers for me a year earlier informed me that they could no longer supply them to me as I had become addicted to them. They told me I needed to go into a detoxification clinic for treatment. I was shattered. What was I going to do? I couldn't be 'normal' without them. How could I possibly tell my husband and family that I was an addict? In reality, I was no different to one . . . I was totally unable to function without them.

That same day, my mother was rushed into hospital for an emergency hysterectomy. Mum had never gone into hospital except to have her babies. I was devastated, scared and desperate. My whole life seemed to be crashing down around me.

That afternoon, I put my two girls down to rest and sat alone in our sitting room. I was terrified and sobbed uncontrollably. For the first time in my adult life, I felt I had my back against a wall. I was desperate. I cried out to God, "If you are there and if you love me like people say you do, than you have to reveal yourself to me because I don't know you. I have to know you. I need your help!"

As I sat there crying for what seemed like an eternity, I heard a knock at the front door. Opening the door slightly, I saw my neighbour standing outside. We had only ever exchanged smiles or the occasional greeting from a distance. We certainly were not what I would term 'friends'. She asked if she could come in and speak to me. I hastily replied she had come at an inconvenient time. I must have looked quite a sight after having been weeping for almost half an hour. She replied, "I believe I've come at exactly the right time and I need to tell you why." I let her in.

She told me as she had been showering at nine o'clock that morning; she had heard very clearly the words, "Go to that girl across the road. She needs your help". She thought she was going crazy so she ignored it. Later on at midday, she heard the words again. Still she ignored them . . . she felt she had never really known me well enough to visit me. Finally, at three o'clock she heard, "If you don't go there now, I will have to send someone else." She immediately knew she was being sent on a divine appointment. She came over to my house at the precise time I had been asking God to reveal Himself to me. She asked me what the problem was. I immediately began telling her about my mother's having surgery and how concerned I was. For the first time in my life, I heard the voice of God in a very gentle, quiet way. His words flooded my mind, "You asked me to reveal myself to you. I have done so. Now, tell her what the real problem is." I was startled by the reality of God's speaking to me. I just blurted it out. "I'm addicted to prescription drugs. The doctor has told me I will have to go into a clinic for detoxification. How am I going to tell my husband and family?" She invited me to go with her to a meeting that evening. I accepted immediately. I was so desperate that, if she had asked me to stand on my head and clap my feet, I would have done so on the turn! I was determined to do anything that would help me in my extreme need.

The meeting, an inter-denominational prayer meeting, was in the hall of the convent I had once attended as a schoolgirl. I went in with my mind filled with scepticism. I really was unsure of what I had let myself in for. Looking around, I saw the singing people with their hands raised, and their faces glowing like angels'. In that room, I sensed the tangible presence of God for the first time in my life. I stood in awe, listening to the beautiful songs and watching the faces around me filled with joy and peace. What had my new friend brought me to? I had never witnessed anything quite so gentle and peaceful in any of the Masses I had attended for so many years. I knew in my heart that it was right. I longed for what these people had . . . the peace, love and joy which seemed to flow from them. However, because I had been so indoctrinated that my religion was the only true one, I was suspicious. But I remained open . . . but alert. I wasn't about to get hoodwinked into any of the cults I had heard about.

Then the music livened up. The people began clapping. This really disturbed me. "Oh dear" I thought, "What is this? Are these the 'happy clappers' I've heard people talk about?" When I reflect on that time, I have to laugh at God's sense of humour . . . just then I looked across the hall. There were five nuns singing, clapping . . . and dancing! I thought, "I'll be okay. The Nuns are here, so I'm safe!" It was such a pity that I had judged every other denomination as being in error until this point in my life.

I listened to the speaker who delivered a wonderful message on God's love. Why had I never heard these things before? Like a thirsty, dry sponge, I soaked in all he said. I experienced such a peace coming over me.

At the end of the service, the speaker asked if anyone would like to ask Jesus Christ into their life as their Lord and Saviour. I thought I had done all that already . . . after all I was a Catholic. I sat glued to my chair. He asked again. I never moved. Then he said, "There is someone here tonight who has cried out to God this very day to reveal Himself to them. They need to be up here." "Wow!" I thought, "God you really did hear my cry. You have sent all these people to help me." I got off my chair and slowly walked to the front to join the other people who had gone forward.

I stood quietly and, after a communal prayer, he asked those who needed specific prayer to stay behind so that he could pray with them afterwards. I stood and waited. He didn't ask me what the problem was. He didn't say or do anything dramatic. He just prayed, "Father, you know the cry of my sister's heart. You know her every need. I thank you that you meet her needs according to your riches in glory, through Christ Jesus your Son. Amen."

That was it! I felt a heaviness lift. A peace flooded my whole being. I never needed to go into the detoxification clinic and never took another tranquiliser from that night. And I had no withdrawal symptoms whatsoever! God was so gracious and merciful to deliver me completely from the addiction to the prescription drugs. He changed me from the inside. I was so thankful to receive His love and Peace. I've had everything the world could offer me but I can truly say, as Paul said, "I count it all dung but for the knowledge of Jesus my Lord."

I have learned that the greater part of happiness or misery depends upon our disposition and not our circumstances, therefore I choose to be content in all situations—Philippians 4:12. If I had never come into my relationship with God, I would have had nothing. He has always been a faithful loving Father and friend to me. From that evening at the convent, when I asked Him to become my Lord and Saviour, I have never felt alone. I have been through many dark, desolate valleys during my journey through life. They have, at times, seemed absolutely hopeless. But I have emerged unscathed and whole in His time and way. He hasn't promised me an easy ride, but He has always ensured my safe arrival. He has enhanced my life, making me a better wife and mother. I am so thankful.

It never ceases to baffle me how complicated some people make Christianity. I am so thankful I lost religion with its traditions, rules and regulations, controversies and schisms. I found, instead, a relationship with a Living God. I now know the joy and freedom of "Christ in me, my hope of glory."

Chapter 5

COPING WITH A CHILD
WITH A.D.H.D AND DYSLEXIA

Vernon and I had two lovely daughters, Lisa and Angelique. We were delighted when our son, Stephen, was born. He was a dark-haired, bonny baby with fine features. He would surely grow into a handsome boy one day.

I decided to bottle-feed Stephen from birth. Oh, how I regretted that decision later when I encountered so many problems with him as an infant! After many sleepless nights and visits to paediatricians, we discovered Stephen had a serious milk allergy. We were a young family struggling to make ends meet on Vernon's salary only. I had to look after our sick baby who was in and out of hospital for some time before he was diagnosed correctly. Life was very difficult at that time. From the time he was born, Stephen seemed to have breathing difficulties. It was very distressing for us as we were unable to find out what was causing these problems. Most nights, I would sleep next him. I was afraid he would stop breathing and die in his sleep. There was so much talk of cot deaths those days. This increased my anxiety. Our baby was seven months old before we had confirmation that he was a serious milk-allergy child.

Once he was diagnosed, we put him on a diet suitable for his condition. He started gaining weight and almost became a normal healthy child.

As young parents, we had so much to learn. Knowledge about allergies and the technology to treat them were certainly not what they are today. Experience was our teacher at that time and a hard taskmaster at that. Our family doctor, who had recently recovered from a serious illness himself, heard what had happened to Stephen. He called me immediately and offered his help. He was so supportive. He personally phoned various baby food manufacturers and walked the supermarket aisles himself to ensure Stephen had a healthy milk-free diet. Until we could work out a proper diet for Stephen, our baby survived on fruit, vegetables, fruit juices and water.

Eventually, our doctor found a formula that Stephen was able to take. Five days of his formula cost as much as our entire weekly grocery bill. Financially, we had to cut many corners to ensure he got his formula.

Stephen blossomed and grew into a lovely child with a kind, sweet nature. We did notice he was extremely active. However, after having two girls, we assumed it was just 'a boy thing'. From fourteen months, he would climb out of his cot and wander around the house at night. He would drag a chair in front of the refrigerator, looking for a snack. When he started doing this, it frightened me. My husband put a lock on Stephen's door to protect him from coming to any harm during the night while we were sleeping.

When he was two and a half years, our son started nursery school. On his first day, I was excited to hear about his first day when I called to collect Stephen from school. My friend, who was the owner of the school, was in a terrible state. She told me that Stephen had been playing in the sandpit a few minutes earlier and had simply disappeared. This was just the beginning of Stephen's many antics. He surely had to be nearby as the school grounds were totally enclosed and secure. I went outside to the sand pit and called him. A little voice came from somewhere above my head, "Mommy." I looked up and held my breath. There he was sitting on the roof of the school! My friend was flabbergasted and went into panic mode. I told her go inside the house. I would get him down. Even though I was horrified to see my precious little boy so high up, I had to be very calm.

"Stephen", I called, "come down slowly, boy. We are going home." I quietly talked him through the descent. He crawled across the roof and climbed down the drain pipe. When he was down, he clung to me, smiling, delighted to see me and totally oblivious of the drama he had just caused. To him, he had done nothing unusual. I was so grateful he had got down unharmed.

The main symptoms of Stephen's A.D.H.D. were his impulsiveness, his easy distractibility, his forgetfulness and his high activity. These all sound like negative attributes. He did, however, bring many positive gifts to our family. It was always exiting to have him around. He livened up every gathering with his energy, creativity and, best of all, his humour. Everyone loved Stephen. He was so lovably mischievous. He had the sweetest smile which lit up his whole face. It was impossible to stay upset with him for long. When he was young, he had the rare quality of owning up when he did anything wrong. He took his punishment like a gentleman and always apologised most sincerely and with much remorse.

It was after Stephen had left nursery school and begun grade school, I could see our son was not at all like his sisters. They had sailed through their school years without problems. Stephen, on the other hand, struggled from day one. By his second year at school, he was diagnosed A.D.H.D. I had never heard of this condition before. His treatment was a matter of trial and error as I truly believe the doctors themselves knew too little about it in those days. And so began many years of visits to paediatricians, psychologists, doctors, occupational therapists, extra lessons, prescribed medications, diets and discipline. It was just as taxing on me as it was on Stephen. I was worn out. I seemed to be running after Stephen constantly, protecting him from other people misunderstanding him and from the dangerous situations he got himself into on a daily basis.

One day I was at the office when I got a call to say our little Jack Russell dog had bitten Stephen. I needed to get home to take him to the doctor. We had acquired this dog recently and, although it was about two years old, it had not been house-trained. This aspect of pet care was a source of great aggravation to me as the delightful task of cleaning up after the dog automatically became my job as soon as the novelty of the new dog had worn off. I had threatened to return the dog to the people who had given her to us if this did not change.

I tore home from the office to find my daughters 'mothering' Stephen. His top lip was bleeding. I was stupefied at what Stephen had done. He had decided the dog should go for a swim with him. So tucking her under his one arm, he dived into the pool and proceeded to swim underwater from one side of the pool to the other—something he enjoyed doing regularly. When he reached the other side, poor Mitsi had gone limp. So, having seen mouth-to-mouth resuscitation demonstrated on a television programme, he decided to give the dog C.P.R. She obviously was in such shock that, when she started breathing again. She bit Stephen through his lip as he was squeezing her nose and blowing into her mouth. She wriggled away and ran for cover under the nearest bush.

I rushed my son to the emergency rooms at the local hospital for treatment. He was to become very well-known at that emergency room over the years. After I had attended to Stephen and knew he was going to be alright, I went home to sort out the dog. We tried everything—food, water, treats and toys. She wouldn't budge and remained under that bush for two days!

I was up at 4am on the second day, having my 'quiet time'. I tried bargaining with God as I prayed, "Please, God, if that dog is alright and comes out from under that bush, I will keep her and not return her to her previous owners." I warmed up some left-over minced beef and went out to her with yet another bribe. I called to her, "Come, Mitsi! There's a good girl." Suddenly, out she strolled from under the bush and gobbled the food down, her tail wagging. All the drama was forgotten! After that incident, she never came and soiled inside the house again. The other children teased Stephen, saying Mitsi had been 'brainwashed' with her swim.

Stephen's pool antics didn't end there. His favourite trick was to dive from the roof of the house into the pool when he had friends over to play. Apparently, he had performed that act many times. His friends were always daring him to do the wildest things. He had no fear whatsoever. One afternoon, I saw it for the first time as I arrived home from work earlier than usual. There he was standing on the roof in a diving position as I drove into the driveway. Helplessly, I watched my young son once again up on a roof. He had not seen the car coming down the road as he was looking in the opposite direction. Seeing my car, he immediately dived from the roof into the pool. The pool had a brick paving surround. One wrong move and he would have landed head first on the bricks. After an extremely harsh reprimand from me, he apologised and promised he would never do it again—I doubt very much that he kept that promise but I couldn't watch him twenty-four hours a day.

Stephen had a BMX bicycle and a skate board and, as might be guessed, he tried every imaginable trick possible on them. One day, he had friends over for a swim. As I came out of the front door to call them in for lunch, I witnessed Stephen doing one of his stunts for his friends. He had found a plank of wood and some bricks and created his own ramp. He then rode like a stuntman towards the ramp at full speed! I watched in horror as he flew through the air on his bike and landed in the deep end of the pool!

During Stephen's childhood, he broke the same leg three times. I cannot count the times I had to rush him to the local emergency centre for stitches after accidents on his bike, skateboard and injuries he received from other wild games he played. When, in his teens, he got his driver's licence, my sleepless nights began! Before he was twenty one years old, he had gone through two motor bikes and three motor cars—accidents, lesser mishaps . . . they were written off, but my son survived!

Once my son got into secondary school, my work was really cut out for me! I realised that I had to help him study in a way he could remember his work. I would summarise his Geography, History and Science books into a question-and-answer format and make him memorise them parrot-fashion. This worked wonderfully. I realised how very bright he really was. It was when it came to writing down the answers that he really struggled. One day, he would do the work perfectly but the very next day, it was as though he'd never learnt how to write. However, if I asked him to answer questions on his work orally, he never made a single mistake.

One day, he had a History test looming. Stephen knew every single date, event and name off by heart. I had got him up at five o'clock every morning for two weeks prior to the test and went over the work until he knew it without making a mistake. The day of the test arrived. Stephen was so excited and confident. He came home absolutely shattered and said, "Mom, I knew all the answers but, when I wanted to write them, I couldn't! I'm sure I've failed!" I gave him a cuddle and re-assured him, if that did happen, I would go and see his teacher and tell her how hard he had studied for his test.

A few days later, he came home so deflated. "Mom, the teacher is so cross with me. Look what she wrote on my test paper—she says I'm going to the headmaster tomorrow!" He was terrified. I looked at his test paper and a righteous anger rose from within me. The teacher had written, "Stephen, you are a very naughty boy. You have not studied at all—you will go to the headmaster tomorrow." I phoned the school and made an urgent appointment to see his teacher in her tea break, as I felt this matter could not wait. I could not allow my son to be sent to the headmaster for punishment which he did not deserve. The teacher was very surprised to hear what I had to say. I asked her, "How many children in your class get up at five o'clock in the morning to learn for two weeks before a test?" Her reply was, "Definitely not one of them." "I beg to differ," I answered. "Stephen has been getting up every morning at five o'clock to study for this exam for the past two weeks. I would be most grateful if you could ask him every question on the test paper and let him answer you orally." She agreed. Stephen was called in and she went through the twenty questions and he answered every one of them correctly. She was shocked and apologised profusely to Stephen. For the remainder of his time at that school, he became her favourite pupil.

Clearly, she could see from this exercise that Stephen needed to be assessed again. After my visit to his teacher, I arranged to have him assessed privately by a professor at the local university. My niece Ingrid was studying for her master's degree in educational phycology and she discussed my plight with her professor. He in turn offered to assess Stephen privately for me. After his assessment, the Professor promised to visit our home the following week with the results. The following week, the school did their standard assessment on Stephen as well. When the professor visited our home, the first thing he said was, "How on earth have you got this child through six years of school?" I told him about the summarising and question/answer technique. "You have done the impossible!" he replied, shaking his head. Both tests proved inconclusive. The professor informed me that Stephen had Attention deficit Disorder with hyperactivity as well as dyslexia and referred him to a remedial school immediately.

Attention deficit disorder (A.D.H.D.) is a family issue. Unlike many other medical problems, it affects everyone in the family daily, in significant ways. It affects holidays and mealtimes and every other part of normal everyday family living. Just as the whole family is affected by the problem, the whole family must be part of the solution. The "balance of attention" is extremely difficult to maintain with an A.D.H.D child and his siblings. Trying to maintain the balance between keeping our son safe and preventing him from always being the centre of attention was hard work. I would no sooner have put out one of his fires than he'd already started another. Trying to handle the situations that inevitably arose from his problems and the resulting tension between Stephen and his sisters was heavy going. Stephen's unrelenting behaviour problems often dominated the family scene. Obviously, this problem affected our marital relationship. As Vernon was always very tired from working long hours, it was easier for him to just give in to Stephen. This caused many an altercation between the two of us. I knew Stephen thrived on discipline and consistency and it annoyed me to see Vernon ignore Stephen's behaviour or give in to his demands just to keep the peace. I would then have to step in and be 'the policeman'. Later, however, after Vernon had committed his life to Christ and we had started praying for Stephen as a couple, he finally acknowledged the need for strict discipline, consistency and boundaries for our son Stephen. Their enforcement began to yield tangible benefits. When Vernon took his headship role, Stephen soon realised that he couldn't play one of us against the other any longer, now that it his parents stood in unity on the matter.

Our precious son suffered so much through A.D.H.D and dyslexia. As his parents, we feel blessed to have been there, to have loved, supported and encouraged our special son throughout his life.

Chapter 6

BUSINESS, CRIME & AIDS
IN THE NEW DEMOCRACY

It was February 1994. With a new constitution in place, the first democratically elected government in South Africa's history would be voted into power in April and take office. In these crucial days of our country's history, Vernon and I were both working in a furniture factory, he as the Production Director and I as Personal Secretary to the Managing Director. This man, who was also owner of the factory, only came into the factory about twice a week. During the two years before the elections and before the factory closed, we encountered serious problems with both the employees and Unions. The workers would go on strike for the pettiest reasons, frequently making violent threats to the supervisors and the White employees.

Despite our pleas for support during these unpleasant times, the owner never felt the situation was serious enough for him to intervene, He would tell us that it was excellent experience for us—'character building' he called it! It may well have been that, but it was playing havoc with our family life. Vernon was working seven days a week and, at one point, didn't have a single weekend or day off in three months. To add to this burden, he received no extra pay for the extra time he had worked.

The demanding workload didn't bother us. We were both very industrious people but, because we had always been very accommodating, humble people, we were easy targets for control and manipulation. The owner was a bully despite his charm. He was also very moody and not easily approachable.

Vernon tried to accommodate the workers' demands as best he could, working with them through the various issues at stake. They were very angry with the owner. Many of them had done private work for him on his home. They had seen his opulent lifestyle. So, they didn't believe him when he came to the factory pleading his inability to increase salaries or to make improvements or purchase new machinery. To the uneducated rural mind, a big house, cars and many possessions spoke of great wealth.

As the situation became more tense, some of the workers became very aggressive. We discovered up to 70% of them smoked marijuana, seeing it as a totally acceptable activity. Our experience told us that their arrogant, aggressive and violent attitudes were linked to their drug habits. Random drug tests showed almost 60% of the workforce was positive with another 20% borderline. We had a massive problem on our hands.

A reliable source revealed that several staff members were selling drugs to our employees and workers in nearby factories. Some of these drug dealers had loaded guns in their lockers. The serious situation demanded attention. The owner reported the matter to the police. The following night, the factory was raided. An intensive search was made and yielded three handguns as well as a large haul of marijuana and other drugs.

When the employees returned to work the next morning, they discovered their lockers had been searched. The drugs and guns were gone. They were furious. The workforce downed tools, demanding a meeting with the owner to discuss what had happened. With two armed bodyguards, he arrived to address the staff. He told the assembled workers he would have nothing to do with the matter. A crime had been committed. The matter was now in the hands of the police. The meeting lasted just five minutes. The owner left the building and returned to his farm. The staff returned to their posts and we all resumed work.

At the end of the work day, we found ourselves locked in the factory. The keys to the premises were missing from my husband's drawer. A staff representative approached Vernon, threatening that, if the drugs and weapons were not returned immediately, our cars would be stoned and the factory torched.

Vernon vainly tried to reason with the workers. He pointed out that he did not have their possessions. It was the police who had confiscated them. They were no longer on the premises. Vernon was drowned out out by chanting of the staff as they 'toy-toyed', demonstrating their disgruntlement in this traditional form of corporate dancing and swaying. Using new tactics in an endeavour to intimidate him, they then turned the issue into something with overt racial overtones.

Vernon offered to ask the police to come and speak to the workforce. This met with a blunt refusal. The situation was becoming extremely volatile. Faced with this intractability, we had no choice but to phone the police. Our lives were now in danger. Vernon instructed me and the other ladies to get under our desks. We were to stay there until the danger has passed.

The frightening sounds of cars and factory buildings being stoned and the insistent rhythmic toy-toying were really chilling. Bricks and rocks were being heaved through the huge pane glass windows. No cars or company vehicles escaped and, in short time, the Delivery Truck was ablaze. We were terrified. The siege seemed to stretch into an eternity. Then we were aware of the building being surrounded by police. All the rampaging staff were taken into custody. Fortunately, no one had been hurt.

Within days of the incident, the factory's owner had decided to close the factory permanently.

We were called in to his office and given one week's notice without a proper severance package. Vernon and I had worked there for seven and five years respectively. We were not surprised at this hasty decision after the two years of on-going staff problems and this recent violence. We were now both without jobs but were nonetheless grateful to be out of a very unpleasant and dangerous situation. Without drastic action like this, we could only envisage matters getting worse. With three children still attending school, we were in our mid-forties . . . a difficult age for White South Africans to find employment no matter how qualified for the job. In the first years of the new democratic South Africa, employers were compelled to employ Blacks only in what was dubbed Affirmative Action, an on-going attempt to redress the injustices of the Apartheid era. The other race groups in the country called it Apartheid-in-reverse in its worst form.

My father phoned me the moment he heard what had happened at the factory. Extremely concerned about our situation, he asked Vernon to call and see him. He offered us an interest-free loan start our own business. This we could start repaying after trading for one year. He knew what a conscientious worker Vernon had always been. He was confident his son-in-law would make a success of his own business.

We were reluctant to accept his offer. We had no idea as to what sort of business to start or how we could ever repay the loan . . . everything around us seemed so insecure and uncertain, but starting our own business was the only way that we, as white South Africans, could survive in the new Democracy. The whites were not alone in being disadvantaged by this new form of Apartheid . . . the Indian and Coloured race groups felt its grip as well. They had been classified as 'Blacks' during the Apartheid era. Now, in the new Democracy, they were 'not Black enough'. Only black African people were considered 'Blacks' and as 'the previously disadvantaged'. The upshot was that they alone were eligible for the benefits Affirmative Action brought.

The new system forced thousands of well-established and flourishing businesses to close their doors. They suffered great staff and financial losses. Every day saw the closure of many Stock Exchange listed companies employing thousands of people.

This precipitated an exodus of White, Indian and Coloured professionals to any country which would accept them and South Africa began to see an alarming 'Brain Drain' leeching the country of much experience and expertise. These emigrants feared for their and their families' futures. It was a tragic time for South Africa that need not have happened. The new democracy had been named the "Rainbow Nation" a term coined by Archbishop Desmond Tutu to describe post-apartheid South Africa. Sadly, the fledgling country was not living up to the promise the name had suggested . . . one where all its citizens would find a place in the sun.

Father had predicted that when Democracy eventually came, the majority of South Africa's population would be a rebellious, arrogant, inexperienced and extremely racist younger generation, despising all race groups but their own. South Africa desperately needed the expertise, skills and experience of all the different race groups. Suitably qualified persons were leaving or being retrenched in their thousands. The majority of their replacements were unqualified, inexperienced, greedy and corrupt. Fraud, corruption, nepotism, illegal strikes and a host of other negative elements bedevilled hitherto successful businesses. The whole country suffered. Government departments, in particular, descended into a shocking state as unsuitable persons were put into positions of great responsibility. Either they had bogus qualifications or none at all. It often took months for this to be discovered. In the meantime, millions of rand had been embezzled and entire departments had been thrown into chaos.

Vernon and I were in our mid-forties—not an easy time to begin again but we had no choice. We had to try and we had to survive. What at that stage was the inevitable outcome of the Aids epidemic meant there was a great demand for coffins. This presented itself as a great business opportunity and so we started a coffin-manufacturing concern. In the first week of operation, Vernon's factory turned out forty coffins. On the Friday morning, a sample coffin wrapped in a blanket, was loaded onto our son's surf-board rack on our car. Vernon then visited four local funeral parlours, each of whom ordered ten coffins for delivery on Monday morning. We were so thrilled. We had sold all our stock! We assumed this surely must be our future.

That week, I was busy finalising the books for the factory where I had previously been employed. I had a phone call from the buyer for a large furniture group with whom we had dealt. He wanted to speak to Vernon and asked what he was doing now the old factory had closed. When I told him, he asked, "Are you joking? Tell him to make me four different sets of coffee tables by Wednesday morning. Ask him to pick me up at the airport at 10am." I couldn't believe what I was hearing. Our new business was operating out of very small and cramped and had a distinctly unprofessional air about it. Our previous employer offered his smart showroom at the old factory for us to display our samples.

On the Wednesday, Vernon met the buyer at the airport and took him to the showroom. When the car stopped, he asked why Vernon had brought him there." He replied "to show you our samples." The buyer's blunt retort was, "I'm not buying a showroom! I'm buying coffee tables! I want to see your place of work".

Vernon sheepishly drove him to the unprepossessing building we called a 'factory' after the samples in the old factory showroom had been inspected. All the tools and machinery were second hand but everything was neat and tidy. The buyer looked at it all with a sharp eye. He questioned our four employees. After a cup of tea, he thanked us and asked Vernon to drive him back to the airport. The only positive feedback we had from him was that he thought the samples 'most satisfactory.'

Chatting about the day's events later, Vernon wasn't very positive. He felt we were perhaps naïve to think that a big Stock Exchange listed company with its sixty four stores would ever consider buying from us. Though we started to nurse a sense of disappointment, we agreed we were glad that we had been afforded the opportunity to tender for the coffee tables. We had been honest and transparent about everything. We didn't expect them to buy from us and decided to carry on making the coffins until something more viable came our way.

The next morning, we received faxed orders for four hundred sets of coffee tables! Our first proper order for our furniture factory! We were ecstatic! Within three months, we had repaid Father the full amount we had borrowed, with interest. He reluctantly accepted. Within a year, the word had got around that we had started a factory. Many of the old staff came seeking employment. Their unions had let them down badly after the debacle over the drugs and firearms. Most of them were now unemployed or destitute. They apologised to Vernon for the way they had treated him and pleaded with him for a second chance. Our children had nick-named their Dad 'the King of Second Chances' . . . he always tried to see the best in people. He gave most of them jobs on condition of 'No Unions'. They all agreed.

Within three years, we had purchased our own factory and things ran well. In our eighth year of operation, we were offered the prospect of manufacturing steel products. With hindsight, I believe we went into this venture too hastily. We had been given a time limit in which to make a decision. We were fearful of losing the contract and skimped on thoroughly researching all the pros and cons of what it would entail. We agreed to take it on. I had a nagging feeling about the whole enterprise from the very beginning. How I wish I had listened to my instincts! We were getting too big far too quickly.

Many of our employees started getting ill and booked off sick for long periods. One staff member after the other was diagnosed as H.I.V. Positive. We had assured them that, if they divulged their status to us, we would stand by them and help them. They were not only scared of losing their jobs but also of being ostracised by their fellow workers. At the time, there was such a stigma attached to Aids. It was particularly so among the Black people as they are very superstitious. Many of them were dying and there was little decent Government health education or treatment for H.I.V. What medical care that was available was horrendous. We had to take our staff to private practitioners at our own expense to have them started on Anti-Retroviral drugs as soon as possible. Our daughter Lisa would sit with them for hours at the hospital. Some of them were so weak, they couldn't even speak. Lisa wouldn't leave until they had been seen by a doctor. More often than not, she was the only White person surrounded by hordes of sick and dying Black people at the clinic.

One after another, the men who worked for us were losing their wives and children to the ravages of the dreaded disease. Vernon was making three or four coffins every month for either some of our employees themselves or members of their families. It was tragic. We were finding it very draining both financially and emotionally but we felt we had to stand by our staff. They had nowhere else to turn.

One of these men, married with two children. gave me permission to share his story. He had disclosed his status to Lisa when he had been first diagnosed. He had seen her helping other employees. He respected Lisa and felt confident to confide in her. Lisa immediately took him to the clinic. He started treatment and was responding well.

A few weeks later, I was attending a conference down the South Coast of KwaZulu Natal. Lisa phoned me in tears. The man had taken a bad turn and needed a brain scan urgently. The local Government hospital wasn't equipped to provide this and so he would have to go to a private hospital. Lisa asked in despair what she should do as the man was desperately ill. I told her to take the money from my personal account and have the scan done. We were going through a very bad patch in the business. I knew it was not in a position to fund the man's treatment. My financial situation was also precarious, but his life was at stake. The scan showed he was extremely ill. Without the information the scan revealed, he would have died within twenty four hours.

Desperately ill, the man remained in hospital for several weeks. One morning, after his recovery, he arrived at the factory with his family. As he came into Lisa's office, he fell to his knees weeping. She was very taken aback. He was generally a very composed and conservative man. He asked for five minutes of our time as he had something he wanted to tell all the staff. When everyone had assembled, he began to speak. He told us that, in all his life, he had never met anyone as kind and good as Lisa. He said God had used her and would carry on using her to help many others. In front of all of us, he said, "Lisa, I see Jesus in you." He believed people were not looking for God in books or in buildings made of bricks. They were searching to see Him in people in their love and care of others. That was how he had found God . . . through the kindness and care Lisa had shown him.

Through her sobs, Lisa said, "You don't know how much this means to me. What you have said has been my life-long prayer that everyone I meet would see Jesus in me and come to know Him." There wasn't a dry eye in the factory that day. Thinking back to those really difficult days, I thank God for the courage and opportunity He gave us to do what was needed to help these people. It was not long after this that the man started attending Bible School. Once he had finished his studies, he became a full time pastor.

I am so grateful that all the original nine employees and their entire their families are all still alive and doing well. This would never have been possible had we not taken them for treatment in time.

Whereas there was much to celebrate on the human side of our business, things were not nearly so rosy on the tough day-to-day running of a concern like ours. About two years before Vernon died, financially things began to spiral out of control at the factory. We kept pouring more and more money into the business with little positive result. It was not the wood factory that was proving our undoing. It was the steel manufacturing side of the operation.

To make things worse, the factory was being paralysed for days on end by power cuts. It was impossible to keep the factory operational without electricity? All our machinery and equipment ran on electricity. We were losing thousands of rand every day in both lost production and in wages needing to be paid despite the factory being at a standstill. Officialdom was deaf to our pleas to do something to alleviate our problems.

When Vernon died, I immediately closed the steel factory. All the employees were transferred to the wood factory. I couldn't afford to take on the extra staff but felt I couldn't abandon them. I poured most of the Insurance pay-outs into honouring the huge deficit which had to be repaid. I realise now I was not very wise in doing this. On the other hand, I felt I did not want to owe money or dishonour my husband's name. In my extremely emotional and vulnerable state at the time, and without anyone strong enough to advise or help me, it was almost to be expected that my decisions would be lacking in sound business sense.

The annual Christmas shutdown began three weeks after Vernon's death. I went into the factory early that morning and was told the total payroll we were paying out that day. My daughter, Angelique felt we needed to get additional security that day. There was a great deal of money on the premises. I agreed. She was so worried at the thought that she took all the cash and locked it in the walk-in safe. Closing day was always busier than usual and everything had to be complete before the annual closure. With all this pressure, we forgot to phone the security company to ask for extra guards. Normally, all our staff were paid via electronic banking. We had taken on a large contingent of casual staff for the last three months of the year and they were to be paid in cash.

The Head Shop Steward came to my daughters and asked if I would address the staff as Vernon had always done in the past. I really didn't want to do this. It had always been my husband's role. I was too physically and emotionally drained to cope with it. The staff representatives came through a second time. I agreed and went through to assembled workforce. As I entered the factory, they were all standing with their heads bowed and their caps in their hands. I spoke to them and then said a short prayer. I asked God to protect them as they went home with their wages, to look after them and their families during the Festive Season and to bring them back safely in the New Year. I then rushed off to take my Mum to a friend's funeral.

I was only gone an hour. I returned to the factory to pay the staff and finish off my paperwork. As I entered the building, I noticed a second hand furniture dealer loading his truck through the front entrance, an entrance not normally used. I had so much on my mind that I didn't question why they were using that door.

I was taken totally by surprise when a short black man walked into my office pointing a gun at me. Grabbing me by the arm, he snarled, "You're the boss! I want the money! Hurry up! Go to the second office on the left."

I thought I was the butt of some sort of joke. How could this man know the payroll was done from that particular office? Just then, one of the ladies in the office screamed, "I haven't got the money! Lisa's got the money!" This was certainly no joke. We were in the middle of an armed robbery. The robbers had come in through the front door. I had little choice but to go with the man. His gun pressed to my head, he dragged me by my arm and pushed me into Lisa's office.

My grandson Jarrod was only six years old at the time. He had just come back from a soccer practice and was squeezing himself through the security gate to visit his Mum in her office. A second robber appeared. Seeing the child climbing through the gate, he grabbed him. He bundled him through to the office, a gun pointing at my grandson's head.

A righteous anger arose within me. My protective instinct outweighed my fear factor. I wrenched myself away from the man who was holding me. Grabbing Jarrod from the second man's grip, I shouted, "Don't you dare touch this child!" I pushed the little boy under his mother's desk. The man from whom I'd just pulled away grabbed me again and, shoving the gun at my head shouted, "If you move again I will shoot you!"

The second gunman lunged towards me aiming his weapon at the other side of my head. He demanded the money. I turned to the first robber, "You are very bad men! I am a widow. God will be cross with you. You must not rob me." He yelled at me, "What did you say?" I said, "In Jesus' name, you must go and leave us alone." By this time, a third man had entered the office. He demanded, "Who is Lisa?" Before my daughter had had a chance to reply, I said, "I'm Lisa." My daughters were pleading, "Mum, don't argue with them! Give them the money! We've just lost our father. We can't lose you too! Please Mum give it to them!"

I glanced down just then. There at my feet lay the petty cash bag under Lisa's desk. It had a mere pittance in it, compared to the payroll. I kicked it in front of them, "Do you want the money? Here! Take the money and go!" The man holding me grabbed the money bag. The three robbers fled the building, with me in pursuit.

To this day, I have no idea what possessed me to chase them. Running down the passage, I spotted the panic button. I stopped in my tracks and pressed it. My hand was still on it when the workers rushed into the offices. The reality of what had just happened began to sink in. I am so grateful to the Lord for his protection that day. I am sure, if any of our work-force had come through to the office while the robbers were still there, someone would have been hurt or killed. I do believe the intruders felt no threat from us because we were all women. I was so thankful that everyone was safe and the payroll was intact.

It was only three weeks later that I was mugged as I came out of the local shopping mall. It happened so quickly that I couldn't brace myself for the assault. A man ripped my gold chain and pendant from my neck and threw me to the ground. As I hit the sidewalk, I felt something wrench in my neck. I phoned the police as soon as I got home. I knew many elderly and vulnerable people frequented that particular mall. I held out little hope of the man being arrested let alone of getting my jewellery back. Much to my amazement, half an hour after my call, the police were knocking at my door. They asked me to come to the station to identify a man they'd arrested and some jewellery. It was the man. He had had my jewellery in his possession when he'd been picked up.

I woke up later that night with both my arms numb. In ten minutes, I had lost all sensation in them. What was happening to me? I was gripped with fear. By 1.30am, I was in the local intensive care unit. In an emergency operation in the early hours of the morning, a cracked vertebrae was discovered. The nerves in my neck were trapped by this . . . all as a result of the mugging.

Shortly after my time in hospital, relations between some of the workers and management at the factory deteriorated. Several of the staff started causing trouble. They informed my daughters that, in the Black African culture it was demeaning for men to take instructions from women. This infuriated me. Early the next morning, I addressed them, "There are only women running this factory since my husband died. I have only kept the business open to keep you all in jobs. So, if your culture doesn't allow you to take instructions from a woman, hand in your notice now. Go and find another job with a man as your employer." It dawned on the workers that they had pushed me beyond the limit. Begging for forgiveness, they apologised to my daughters and me and went back to work.

Pressures continued to mount and the resulting stress weighed me down in my spirit For a whole year before I eventually decided to close the factory, I had such a longing to be released from this enormous responsibility. I had enrolled in a First Aid and Home Caring course which I hoped I would one day be able to use. I had a deep desire to care for the elderly. Suddenly, in the June, huge orders began to pour in! This would surely turn things around. At last, I saw light at the end of this dark tunnel I had been in for almost five years. Unfortunately we didn't have the capital to meet the challenge and no large credit facilities to purchase the materials required to meet the orders.

My mother had always been my mentor and confidante. Immediately, she offered to help. Without my knowing, my daughters had spoken to a close friend who also agreed to help. It was unbelievable how everything was seeming to 'fall into place'.

We started manufacturing for delivery from August through to December. The first blow came in the first week of October. A fax arrived cancelling more than half the orders. The reason given was the worldwide credit crisis. We were told that if we sent the orders, they would not be accepted. What could we do under these impossible conditions? Ours was a small family business. Our customer was a major company. We would never have the resources to fight them legally. They could afford the best legal teams in the country. We tried every avenue to save the business. Eventually, after submitting our Financials to our Auditors, we were advised that we had no option but to close the factory immediately. It would be illegal to trade under these circumstances. I was shattered. We had accepted financial aid on the strength of those orders. Now, we were left with a factory full of products and materials. We had no choice but to close the business. Integrity had always been one of the values on which I had based my life. To honour my commitments in both my personal and business capacities was a given. Now, I found myself in a dark tunnel with no glimmer of light at the end of it.

As always, my mother was my rock at through that testing time. I was devastated at thought that so much money, on the strength of the orders, had been put into the business for materials. How would I ever repay it? Then there was my friend who had so generously helped in our time of need. They too would have to be repaid. If I had not known God as my provider and not had such love and support from my family during this time, I am sure I would have ended my life.

Those were the worst and best days of my life. God met me in that dark hour. More importantly, He had already begun preparing me for the radical changes I was about to undergo. People ask whether it is possible to find God in the midst of brokenness, loss and pain. They struggle with whether He may be preparing them for a life of new beginnings. They find it difficult to believe that fresh hope, love, strength and laughter might be their lot again. I can assure them that they most definitely can. I did. He has no favourites. What He's done for me, He will do for them. They need to reach out in their desperation and grasp His hand. He's the only one who will never leave or forsake them.

Survivors and overcomers aren't those who never stumble, fall or fail. I'd failed so often. I was only capable of rising yet another time through His grace, strength, wisdom and love. I rose again with a new strength. And so can anyone who reaches out to God. In that dark hole of despair and great burden, His loving arms reached down to me. He relieved me of my crushing burden. He then led me to a place of peace and new beginnings in so many areas of my life. As people in the midst of despair put their trust in Him, I know they will find the same hope and freedom I found. As they seek Him, they will find Him. As they knock, He will open the door. As they ask, He will answer. He is a faithful, merciful, loving God to All who call on Him

Chapter 7 ═══════════════════════

LIFE WITH A RECOVERING
DRUG ADDICT

It was very evident from an early age that my son Stephen would live a life filled with challenges, both for him and for our whole family. When one member of the family is battling with a serious problem like addiction, no member of the family escapes the heartache and pain attached to it. Through my writing about those times, I have endeavoured, over the past few years, to remember him as he was before we lost him. What I mean was not a physical death but the dramatic change in our son when drug abuse forced its ugly way into all of our lives. There are mini-deaths experienced over and over again through the relentless highs and lows of addiction. Stephen went through the rollercoaster of binges, remorse, relief, possible rehabilitation, and short periods of peace always followed by yet another relapse.

Stephen had a great sense of humour and brought this wonderful gift of his into our family situations in an amazing way that we miss so much today. Although he is very good looking, he sadly has a low self-esteem. His underachievement at school bred a great sense of inferiority in our son. In an attempt to compensate for this, he often exhibited an air of superiority which gave people the impression that he was arrogant and had great self—confidence. Nothing could have been further from the truth. I believe his life of addiction was an attempt to deal with his underlying negative feelings of low self-esteem. The drugs offered him the deceptive promise of a sense of belonging. His friends loved him and he loved them . . . they accepted each other unconditionally as they all shared the same problems.

I am firmly convinced the addictive gene was in him when he was born. One will never know why it skips some generations or siblings and affects others. What is certain is that, somewhere down the line, the susceptibility definitely does carry through the genes. I can say this because his father and I both have some family members with addictive tendencies.

Before our shocking discovery of Stephen's addiction, we would never have believed this could happen to one of our children. They were all loved, nurtured and wanted in exactly the same way. Having said that, I believe we probably handled Stephen the wrong way. We only found out that he was taking drugs after experiencing much inexplicable loss and heartache. Unfortunately, neither he nor we realised the problem was so serious until his actions began to work out their ugly consequences on him and on us.

Through this painful learning process, I made a very interesting discovery . . . most families have addicts in their families just like we have in ours. The majority of them manage to conceal it, whether the addiction is to alcohol, street drugs, gambling, prescription drugs, over-the-counter drugs, pornography, sex, perfectionism, sport, work, eating or to starving oneself . . . and these are only a few of the addictions that can gain a stranglehold. People who are trapped by them fall into two categories: the first group are able to conceal their lifestyle to a certain extent. They may be able to get up the morning after having indulged their particular weakness the night before and can function normally. Their problem doesn't affect their work, family or social life too adversely. The second group of addicts only need a single night of indulgence or a few days of binging to leave them incapable of functioning for days, and sometimes weeks, on end. Unfortunately, Stephen fell into the second category.

I saw the many warning signs that something was amiss. When I voiced my fears to Vernon, he felt I was over-reacting. By the time

Stephen began his perilous journey into the world of drugs, Vernon had committed his life to Christ. He was attending church with me but his spiritual growth had been limited. The new business we had started was consuming an enormous amount of his time, energy and attention. He spent very little time reading God's Word or in prayer. Our prayer time together as a couple and a family every morning before Vernon's leaving for work was the sum total of his weekday spiritual time. When the crisis of Stephen's addiction hit our family, we were not in total unity as husband and wife. The result was that, once again, Stephen used the situation, as he had done with his A.D.H.D., to manipulate us and play us off against each other. By the time the situation had seriously deteriorated and the Law had intervened, Vernon began to seek God more diligently. We began dealing with the situation as a couple. Before this, I always had had to deal with most of the repercussions of Stephen's behaviour on my own. For at least two years, I fought on in this emotionally and physically draining battle. I harboured feelings of resentment and started to see myself as a martyr. I eventually had to take myself in hand. I was amazed when I realised these two aspects of my reaction to Vernon's abdication of responsibility were actually sinful. I begged God to forgive me and help me. That was the turning point when Vernon made the decision to take on his fatherly responsibility and became more involved.

At the same time as I was struggling on my own with Stephen's problem, was on the receiving end of verbal abuse and cruelty from both friends and family. It was very painful for me to hear, "You're living in denial! He's got you fooled! He's taking you for a ride! Write him off! He's rotten! He needs to be behind bars." People flung very insensitive comments at me: "You'd all be better off if he took an overdose. He'd be doing you, himself and society a favour". These were most painful words for me as his mother to hear. It grieved me to know what these people really thought. I had thought they knew and loved me.

To stand by helplessly and watch him self-destruct has been almost impossible to bear at times. By turns, I've been angry, hurt, abused mentally and emotionally—dealing with the demands of his addicted life-style has often left me physically exhausted. The problems flowing from it have cost me enormous amounts of money to settle the debts he's incurred, to make good loss and damage of so many kinds, to pay rehabilitation fees and for medical and psychological assistance.

Stephen has had a very unhappy life since he fell into the jaws of this addiction. He has been rejected by friends, family and society. He has been shunned, ignored and ostracised. He is no longer welcome among his family and has missed many important family functions and Christmas gatherings. He is forever losing all his belongings. He's been penniless, homeless, and has not been able to hold permanent employment. He has slept in parks and in doorways. The sad list goes on and on . . .

Despite his being a bright, good-looking boy, Stephen's under-achievement at school, due to his learning difficulties, gave him a low self-esteem. He was on medication prescribed by specialists for nine years. When he was sixteen, he was suddenly taken off them. I believe this created the platform for his life of addiction. The medication he had been on for all those years was a known stimulant. The specialists never once suggested weaning him off them. The decision to stop the medication came at a day's notice. Back then, there wasn't the knowledge there is today about the side effects of the sorts of medication Stephen was taking, about how patients need to be weaned off the drugs. Within six months of abruptly stopping them, our very vulnerable son became addicted to an infinitely more dangerous stimulant—cocaine.

Stephen was sixteen years old and in a private school when we started noticing changes in him. From being a gentle, kind, caring and transparent boy, our son became a quiet, secretive, moody, angry, lying and manipulative person. He began inviting strange people we'd never met before around to our home, introducing them as his new friends. Before embarking on his life of drugs, he had thoroughly enjoyed his family and home life. Now, he became very untidy and stopped caring about his hygiene and appearance. His school work took a marked downward turn and it was a struggle to get him to do his homework.

The next bombshell came when he announced he was leaving school. We tried all kinds of incentives to encourage him to finish his schooling.

Eventually, it was Stephen who won the battle. We were worn out from the constant arguing with him. He had abandoned all pretence of doing any school work. We decided to take him into the factory we owned and train him in the various departments. We really believed this would make him happy and that he would settle down. Stephen was delighted. Parents so often believe they are doing the right thing for their children but, I now have to acknowledge this move was yet another big mistake. Vernon and I should have stood firmly against his leaving and made him complete his schooling.

No sooner had he started working at the factory, than he discovered very quickly how he could earn some extra money to support his underworld social lifestyle. He started stealing furniture from the factory and selling it to pawnbrokers and second-hand shops. If he had a delivery of three bedroom suites, he would sneak one or two extra suites onto the truck. He would then pocket the money for the extras he sold. He was our son, after all! Again, we made another great mistake on our part for trusting him. We should have known to be more vigilant. We soon learned the hard lesson that a person with an addiction problem cannot be trusted. The sad truth was that we had to learn the hard way.

After a while, Stephen began to disappear for days on end. I would drive the deserted streets at 2 am, desperately searching for him. Most times, my searching was to no avail. Eventually, after several days, he would come home, filthy and exhausted. How he didn't die during one of those terrible periods over the years, only God knows. So often, after these times when he was deep into the downward spiral of drug abuse, I could expect visits from the 'debt collectors'. These unsavoury characters would call at the factory to say that Stephen owed them enormous amounts of money. We helped him pay his debts as we feared these people would harm him. Two of his close friends had 'supposedly' committed suicide. We understood that these sad events were very clear messages to the addicts in general: "Pay up or you will go the same way." Stephen was under no illusion that his friends had died because they could not pay their debts to the dealers. After their deaths, our son was terrified. He managed to live a relatively normal home life with his family . . . until the next time. What it was that triggered his disappearances varied, but it always happened suddenly and when we least expected it. The perplexing thing was that he always seemed at his happiest just before he left. We were never prepared and always were caught off guard. When he had run out of money, he would start trying to pay his debt by giving the dealers his mobile phone as a down payment. The rest of the debt he had incurred was put 'on account'. This they would come to claim from us a few days later.

We learned very quickly to leave the police out of the situation and handle things ourselves. On three occasions, we asked for help from the police. There was none forthcoming. We had no choice but to protect Stephen ourselves as best we could. The only way we could do that was to pay his debts or try some other new form of treatment.

Stephen has taken 'full responsibility' for his addiction. He has often said to me, "Mom, I can't blame anyone else—I was stupid to ever start. Nobody forced me—they might have made it available, but I did it myself." He has been in and out of various treatment centres but, sadly, he has never seen any rehabilitation course through to its end. He has always claimed he felt better after two or three months and decided he could do the rest on his own. Recently, he went to spend time on a rehabilitation centre on a farm run by a Christian organisation. For the first time, he seemed to be learning and understanding more about his problem. He began to understand why he had always struggled so much with the addiction. He realised he had not been not born a bad person, but that he had a predisposition to harm himself and those near and dear to him. We too began to get a greater understanding of addiction through the folk running the farm than we had through any of the other places he had been in before. Unfortunately, as had happened so many times before, Stephen took himself out of this rehabilitation centre claiming he felt better after just two months. This was totally against the organisation's advice that he would be better helped if he remained there for at least eighteen months.

One Sunday evening, he disappeared, just like so many times before. The family searched for him for days. His friends had given him refuge. My son-in-law eventually found him, hiding in a cupboard at one of these friends' house. He was perilously close to death. His skin was a ghastly greyish blue. He was in a terrible physical condition and we rushed him to hospital. He returned to the farm for treatment. This time, he stayed for six months, the longest he has ever stayed anywhere. He is now working for one of his friends. As I live so far away from him, I make a point of speaking to him on the phone every week. He knows I love him and is always so happy to hear from me. Every night before I go to sleep, I thank God for getting my son through another day.

When I began this particular chapter, Stephen had moved back home with his family and started a new job, He was so happy to be back with those who loved him. Everyone said it was such a wonderful month they had with him. They would call and tell me, "It's been the happiest time we've had with Stephen in years. We really believe this is it. He has beaten it!" That too was short-lived. He disappeared a month later.

Many people have asked me about Stephen's claim that he hates having this problem. They question why, if he hates it so much, can't he stop? They pontificate, "He has made his choice and must reap the consequences of his wrong choices." Even though I do not accept this as being true in all cases of addiction, I simply do not have a pat answer as to why our son was not able to make what seems to others as a clear and easy choice. Who, in their sane mind, would choose this pointless and debilitating lifestyle if there was an easy way out? The majority of these self-appointed experts base their judgements on minimum personal knowledge of my son's character and what he had to contend with. Yet they constantly lecture me on to how to handle his problem. They need to walk in my shoes for a few months. Then they can come and share their advice. I have been told to throw him out and have nothing to do with him. They call their proposed solution 'Tough Love.' I have tried it. It only made him far worse. I have attended Tough Love groups for years. I have attended every lecture possible on my son's problem. I don't doubt that these may have been effective in some cases and helped some people. It quite clearly wasn't the answer to our problem—I wish it had been. It's so easy to speak from a position of superior knowledge when one has not suffered the pain of a loved one being locked in a seemingly endless struggle and which seems so hopeless at times.

Many times over the years, Stephen has come to me and hugged me saying, "Mom, thanks for never giving up on me." In those brief special moments, I see my real wonderful son and trust that I will one day see him normal. His family has lived with this great challenge for so many years. Through it all, we have loved each other very dearly. We long to see Stephen free of this bondage and able to live a normal life. I will never give up doing all I can to see him able to enjoy that freedom. Though I am not an expert on the subject, I have gained enormous insight into the world of drug abuse through living with an addict for eighteen years. No book could ever have taught me what I've learned. More importantly, I have gained understanding, compassion and the will to never give up or judge others with similar problems.

I can't make Stephen trust God. I can't force him to go for help or change him. Nonetheless, I do know that God is the very best chance he has of helping him do all these things. He loves his family dearly and I hope that he can eventually make up for lost time and opportunities in the future. Having said all this I still love him, and will keep trying, in the hope that one day he will be free. Because I know my own son so well and because I know my God so well, I will continue to trust Him, believing that He will help Stephen. I have great faith that he will one day be free to live a more peaceful and normal life.

I feel very privileged to be able to share my experiences through Stephen's struggles and what I have discovered about addiction. I hope it will be of help and encouragement to other families facing similar challenges. I don't have the solution to the problem. What I can do is share my coping mechanisms, the greatest of which is my unconditional love for my son. I will never give up hoping that one day Stephen will trust God completely and be free to enjoy a normal life. It has been a long journey of love, hope, despair and endurance. I want to know that, when I have completed this journey with him, no matter what the outcome, that I did everything possible to help him. With God's help, I sincerely hope to accomplish this.

Chapter 8

WHEN GOODBYES COME TOO SOON

Shortly before he died, Vernon and I celebrated our 35th wedding anniversary. Over several years before his death, I saw him change greatly. When people have been married as long as we had, they might have attributed this to 'male menopause' or 'mid-life crisis.' Every aspect of my husband's life seemed to undergo significant change during that time. My greatest regret was not being aware of how really ill he was. From time to time, he mentioned in passing that he seemed to be losing his sense of balance. I presumed it was a middle ear infection or vertigo. Vernon was one of the most difficult people to persuade to visit the doctor. Sadly, he wouldn't go to my doctor, whom I am sure would have diagnosed his illness much earlier.

Two years before his death, he had a bad fall and needed a shoulder replacement. He was unable to function normally for three to four months after surgery. He started to experience many bouts of depression, something he never had to deal with before. He also complained of constantly feeling tired and of buzzing noises in his ears. His doctor kept telling him he was suffering from stress. Until that time, Vernon's family had been a priority in his life but now he started going out alone every night. That was something he had never done before. He had always been a balanced, wise person and never made any major business decisions unless we were both in agreement. Now, he began making very irrational business decisions. He would get very angry if I opposed ideas of his which I felt were clearly not right. At home, he would lose his temper over the pettiest things . . . he would complain the television was too loud even though the volume was set on normal.

I had discussed Vernon's personality change and his other symptoms with my doctor. He was very concerned that my husband may have had a minor stroke or have a brain malfunction of some sort. Even though this worried me terribly, I had to be so tactful about asking Vernon to go for a second opinion about the symptoms he was presenting. He got very angry and refused.

Over a period of more than two years, he became increasingly violent in his speech and behaviour. I became scared of him. Rather than argue, I would keep quiet and give in to his demands. His wrong decision-making in the business became more frequent. He would fly into a towering rage if I dared oppose any of his decisions or tried to reason with him. I dreaded having to discuss anything with him.

Vernon developed a persecution complex and was convinced his family were all conspiring against him. Our children were frightened, confused and angry as they watched the change in the Dad they adored. Even though they loved him, they couldn't understand how I tolerated the violent man he'd become and the abuse I was subjected to daily.

After thirty-five years of marriage, I tried to be understanding and cover up my spouse's shortcomings. For about four years after his death, I regretted not having been more forceful about making him get a second opinion. I felt I had been a coward and should have been brave enough, even in the face of his abuse, to insist that he saw another doctor.

In the middle of 2003, he moved into our spare room as all night one of his legs jerked involuntarily whilst he was sleeping. I was being kicked about twenty to thirty times a night. My legs were covered in bruises. I knew he couldn't control it, but if only he had gone for help.

To complicate things, about two years earlier, he had been diagnosed with sleep apnoea, a condition caused by an obstruction in the airway and which resulted in his stopping breathing for ten seconds or more. He slept with a C.P.A.P machine to help with his breathing. Being in his own bed in a separate room ensured we both had a better night's sleep. It really saddened me that he had to sleep on his own as we had always had a good marriage. I would feel so alone and would lie awake at night pleading with God to help me to help him. Often I would cry myself to sleep.

Vernon would constantly complain of his legs going numb. He said it felt as though electric shocks were shooting through them. As time went by, his hyper-sensitivity to any noise increased. He said it made his head ache.

On our 35th anniversary, we had a dinner party at home with friends. I was not feeling well at all but didn't want to spoil the evening. Vernon was his 'old self' and was so happy that day. I was so happy he seemed to be his old self for a change even if I feared the change would be short-lived. I couldn't eat. I felt so weak and was nervous, because I felt so poorly. I ended up excusing myself from the table and going to bed. Vernon was so caring and worried. He knew I must have been feeling very ill to have gone to bed when we had guests, particularly on such a special occasion. He sat and stroked my head until I fell asleep, telling me how he couldn't bear to see me like this and how much he loved me. It was so nice, even in that state I was in, to have my loving, caring husband at my side once again.

The next morning, I was rushed to hospital. After three days in isolation and a battery of tests, I was diagnosed with Hepatitis A. After a ten day stay in hospital, I spent two weeks at Mum's with her overseeing my recovery. I was as weak as a kitten and needed to rest. Vernon visited me often and was attentive and thoughtful. It was as though my old husband had returned. He said he was missing me so much. I decided to go back home.

The following year, 2004, Mum and I had booked to go to Ireland to visit my niece. After my ill health, the specialist encouraged me to go on the trip. He insisted I travel with a wheelchair because of the long distances in the International airports. Vernon hated flying and even though I wanted him to come with us, he declined. He was happy for Mum and me to go. We had been in Ireland for just over a week when

I got a call from my daughter, Lisa, "Mum, something strange has happened to Dad!"

Vernon had gone to the local supermarket which he had been frequenting for thirty years. He had been found standing in the middle of the shop, crying and asking people where he was. He couldn't remember why he was there and didn't even know his name. Fortunately, the lady serving on the deli counter had recognised him. She'd phoned Lisa who had come and fetched him immediately. He was taken to hospital and a psychiatrist was called in.

That evening, when I phoned from Ireland, the psychiatrist told me he thought Vernon was suffering from 'burnout'. I told him I thought he was wrong. I believed there was something far more seriously wrong with my husband. I pleaded with the psychiatrist to do a brain scan . . . there had been such drastic changes in Vernon over the past two years. He laughed at me and said, "I know my job, my girl" to which I replied, "I'm certainly not disputing that, but I think I know my husband better than you and I believe he is seriously ill". He asked me to give him time to investigate further.

Over the next three days, I tried without success to contact this doctor several times from Ireland. I decided to fly back to South Africa. My younger sister would accompany Mum home later. Before I got home, Vernon was discharged from hospital. He finally made an appointment to see my doctor. I was thrilled to hear this. I was confident that he would get to the bottom of my husband's problem. Vernon opened up to him in the most wonderful way and, before he left, he asked the doctor to pray for him. My doctor then spoke with Vernon's doctor. Further tests and brain scans were done. I felt relieved that, at last, something concrete was being done.

When my doctor later told me about Vernon's visit to his surgery, he told he had never met a more humble person and one that loved his family so much. Vernon said he regretted not having gone to see him sooner and was much happier after that visit. I know subconsciously he knew there was something seriously wrong with him.

When I got back to South Africa, I was met by a very excited husband, so happy to have me home. Fortunately, during those few days away, I had regained much of my strength and felt much better. I needed to be strong to face the challenges that lay ahead.

As soon as I set eyes on Vernon at the airport, I knew something was seriously wrong . . . his head was so swollen. Could nobody see what was happening to this poor husband of mine? Even our children said they hadn't noticed anything amiss until I pointed it out to them.

The doctor had given instructions that Vernon was not to drive a car until further notice. I hadn't been home three hours when he wanted to go out on his own—in the car! I said earlier Vernon had always loved being at home with his family . . . now it seemed he wanted to run away from us all the time. When I tried to gently tell him he had been advised not to drive, he flew into a tantrum, telling me there was nothing wrong with him. He demanded the keys which I had hidden away safely. I tried to distract him by asking him to come and have a rest with me. He turned on me and got very abusive. Not knowing quite what to do, I went through to the bedroom and lay down on the bed, hoping Vernon would follow me and forget about going out in the car. Totally out of control, he started yelling at me and hurling things around the room. He was completely impervious to any attempt to calm him down or rationalise with him . . . he simply would not listen. He then started throwing the items at me. My son and daughter came to my rescue. They tried to get Vernon out the bedroom, but he just roughly pushed them aside. Throughout our married life, I had been the one person he would always listen to when he was upset . . . now he was totally unapproachable and irrational. It felt as though I was talking to a total stranger. His behaviour was that of a demented person. I was terrified of what he might do next. It grieved the children to see their father, who was always known as the 'Gentle Giant' acting this way. I locked myself in the bedroom and phoned my brother to come and help us. I was drained and tired. My body ached. How could I help my poor husband? I felt so utterly alone and helpless.

Vernon had always had a very good relationship with my brother. When he began ranting and raving, Derrick put his arm around his shoulder and gently led him to the bedroom. He sat quietly talking to him. I could hear loud wracking sobs coming from the room and Vernon saying in desperation, "Derrick, I love my family. What's wrong with me? Why am I like this? Please have me locked away. I am so scared I am going to hurt Angela and the children." It tore at my heart to have to hear my husband speaking like this. Derrick phoned the neurosurgeon who told him to take Vernon to the hospital immediately. By Monday morning, brain tests and an MRI scan had been done. The psychiatrist phoned me with the bad news, "I am so sorry. You were right your husband is a very ill man—in fact he is terminal."

I was shattered. Nonetheless, at last I knew what was wrong with my husband. A friend of Derrick's was the radiologist in attendance. He was very kind and honest with Vernon and me. Vernon wanted to know the truth. The radiologist told us the tumours were so large they would take Vernon's life within three months. When he spoke to me alone, he said, "You need to prepare yourself, Angela. It may be much sooner than that. It's all over his brain."

Little did I realise just how soon it would be. Vernon was so very brave. He insisted that we go home. When we got there, he asked me to bring all the files with our insurance policies and legal papers. He asked me to phone our broker and lawyer so that they could come to the house. He wanted to discuss everything with him. He sorted out all the paperwork so that I would have no problems after he had died. I felt sick to my stomach, watching and hearing all this going on in such a matter-of-fact fashion.

I will always be so grateful for what Vernon did that day. When I did lose him, his meticulous attention to all these vital affairs relieved me of what could have been so stressful. We had often talked about our growing old together, joking about what it would be like. In our wildest dreams, we had never imagined we would ever have to face the loss of one of us in our early fifties.

After this dreadful news had been broken to us, I hardly slept that night. I tossed and turned, wondering how I was going to carry on my life without Vernon. I was scared and broken-hearted. I couldn't let him know about the emotions I was battling with. He had so much to deal with himself. I had to take control of my feelings and thoughts and be strong for him.

How would he cope, knowing he was going to die? What was he thinking? What was he feeling? He seemed very calm and put on a brave front as he waited to go into hospital for a biopsy to diagnose the lethal tumour that was going to steal him from the children and me.

The operation was scheduled for early the next morning. He was admitted that afternoon. The visitors' room was full of friends and family. Everyone loved Vernon. He was so delighted to see Mum, who had returned from her holiday in Ireland. He loved her dearly and had a wonderful relationship with her. His two godchildren, my nieces, Maysie and Candice were living in London at the time. They took the first flight back home to see him and support the family.

Vernon seemed more peaceful in the hospital. He was delighted to see everyone. He showed such courage and selflessness, thinking of everyone else and how we were coping. The children felt so cheated at the awful thought of losing their beloved Dad so soon. They never showed their sadness at all when they visited him. He had a wonderful sense of humour and they joked and laughed to distract him from the seriousness of the situation.

At 5am the next morning, Stephen went to the hospital to help his Dad shower and to be able to spend time with him before his biopsy. After the very stormy relationship the two of them had had through the years of Stephen's addiction, it was good for him and Vernon to have had this time alone. Another MRI scan was going to be done before he went into theatre. Stephen stayed with him. I was glad his son was with him in his greatest time of need. Stephen came home sobbing and so remorseful for all the years of pain and disappointment he had caused his father. He was inconsolable for hours. Now we could do nothing more but wait. Back at the hospital, we waited for him to come out of surgery. It seemed like an eternity before I was called me to go and see him.

Vernon's head was swathed in bandages, his eyes swollen and shut. There were tubes and apparatus all over him. I gently held his hand, "Vernon, can you hear me? Do you know who I am?" He squeezed my hand and gave me a thumbs-up with the other hand, "Yes, of course I know you! You're my darling wife." I was engulfed in a flood of tears of sadness and joy . . . I was so happy he knew me. Then, the children greeted their Dad. Vernon responded perfectly, knowing each of them by name.

He started having seizures of varying intensity. It was so painful to see him going through all this horror, but we knew he needed us with him. We had to put our feelings aside and be there for him. We didn't leave his bedside until the staff asked us to leave in the evening. We had talked to him and he answered us from time to time. As that long day wore on, he stopped talking altogether. I am sure he was in a coma.

The hospital staff removed most of the tubes and machines, leaving only the oxygen, blood pressure gauge and one other monitor going. I would never see him open those beautiful blue eyes again. The results came back . . . the tumour was a Glioblastoma, the most aggressive primary malignancy in humans. There was nothing more which could be done for him. The tumour covered 90% of his brain.

When the two nieces arrived from London, there was a noticeable change in Vernon's vital signs as they spoke to him. I am sure he could hear them and was happy they were there . . . he was deeply fond of them.

The doctor eventually stopped the medication that was preventing his brain from swelling. He told us it was only prolonging the inevitable. This was indescribably difficult news for the family. We were being offered us no hope whatsoever. The hospital staff started administering Morphine. I hated the idea of this, but I had no choice in the matter. The surgeon attending him had an awful bedside manner and barely spoke to me or discussed anything with me when he visited Vernon.

Every evening, my own doctor would phone me to say he had stopped by on his way home from his surgery to see Vernon. He believed Vernon could hear everything he said to him, saying that, usually, the hearing was the last sense to go when a person was dying. He advised us to keep talking to and encouraging Vernon on our visits. He promised he would look at his charts and tell me in layman's terms about Vernon's condition. Most importantly of all, my doctor told us he was not in pain and was very peaceful. This was such a great comfort and encouragement to me in those last days. I will always be grateful for my doctor's love and care for our family during that incredibly difficult time.

The days dragged by agonisingly slowly. Each night, I would drop into bed like a limp rag. I cried myself to sleep, desperately hoping that I would wake up and find this was only an awful dream. Every morning, I would rush to the hospital, always hoping for a miracle . . . but it was not to be. I would sit at Vernon's bedside, telling him about the grandchildren and their latest antics and giving him general news and messages from well-wishers.

Our two little grandsons were begging to see their Papa. As they were so young, Lisa and Marc didn't want to bring them to the hospital. Someone suggested that each of us needed to have private time with Vernon and that we should bring the children to see him. Nine days after his surgery, we each spent our private time with him. Lisa and Marc brought Jarrod and Cody, his two little red-heads. They lay on their Papa's chest as they had done so often in the past. The machines he was hooked up to next to his bed started re-acting, lines and numbers changing. I am sure Vernon knew the little ones were there. We were all so glad they had come to spend time with their Papa.

On the tenth day, the 4th November 2004, we were back at the hospital as usual. By 2pm, Angelique and I were exhausted. Lisa and Stephen stayed at their Dad's side to give us a chance to go home to have an hour's rest. We had almost got there, when my mobile phone rang. Lisa told us to come back to the hospital immediately. Vernon's blood pressure and heart rate were dropping rapidly. We turned the car around and raced back to the hospital. We tore down those all too familiar stairs to the Intensive Care Unit.

When we walked into Vernon's ward, the curtains around his bed were drawn. Immediately, I knew he had gone. What we had been dreading had finally happened. No matter how prepared someone may think they are, no matter whether they believe they have all the facts, nothing prepares them for the moment when what they have been bracing themselves for actually happens—no amount of preparation readies one for losing a loved one. Vernon had died with Lisa and Stephen at his side about two minutes before we arrived. I had such a deep sorrow that I hadn't been with him when he'd slipped away. He looked was so peaceful as he lay there. His cheeks were still pink. I kissed him goodbye. My precious husband of 35 years was pain free and at peace at last. For him, this was a release and a blessing. For us, our pain and loss was about to begin.

For days on end, people brought flowers and meals. One of Vernon's suppliers brought an enormous white floral arrangement to his office. Our employees lit a candle which burned next to the flowers for several days. His office looked like a shrine. The employees passed it with great reverence, taking their caps off and bowing their heads. He had been a good employer and they mourned his passing.

Time passed. I was occupied with trying to exist from one day to the next. I was far too busy to feel sorry for myself or get depressed. There were too many people depending on me to be strong. God clearly demonstrated His love and faithfulness to me through His Word by 'never leaving or forsaking me'—Hebrews 13:5 and caring and guiding me as a widow—'He is a judge of the widow'—Psalm 68:5. Many times I had difficult decisions to make and struggled with the business and Stephen. It was during those times He remained faithful to His Word and guided and protected me through some very frightening situations.

It's been 7 years since I lost Vernon. He will always have a very special place in my heart that no-one else will ever fill. I shall always be grateful for the courage, strength and peace my Loving Heavenly Father gave me at the time of Vernon's untimely death. The love of God and that of others helped me cope with the loss of my husband.

Chapter 9

I STOPPED JUDGING
AND BECAME A SEE-THROUGHER

My beautiful niece Maysie had come out of the closet, disclosing she was gay. I was shocked, disappointed and angry with her when she told me. I couldn't believe or accept it. Thinking back, I see how often we make faulty judgements based on minimal information. I have been humbled by the realisation that my careless judgement so often could have been so destructive, if it were not for God's intervention. The relationship between my niece and me was very strained for a few years until God revealed to me how very judgemental I had been. I underwent a complete change of heart.

She had been living in England for about seven years when her older brother was killed in a car accident. She came back to South Africa for his funeral. Shortly before his death, I had read an article in a Christian magazine which really struck me. It spoke so clearly of the need for all true Christians to be 'see-throughers'. What the author meant was that we should see through the labelling systems of the world to the hearts of people, and love them as God loves them. Whether they are of a different faith or culture, gay or straight, fat or thin, ugly or pretty, addicts or not, we are to love them unconditionally just as He loves us. This brought me up short as I had always regarded myself as a good upstanding Christian. I was sure I had always loved everyone as I should. I was extremely grateful when I realised I was being given an opportunity to repent of my spiritual pride, my judgemental attitude and lack of true Christian love. I was being offered a chance to learn how to become a see-througher.

Maysie was one of the first people that I learned to love this way. I am so glad I embraced this revelation and began to live it. I have so many regrets as to how initially I had judged her and wasted three precious years. Before her 'coming-out', we had been very close. I was truly sorry for not being the aunt and Godmother I should have been during that time. I felt I had not been there for her when she needed me the most. After she had arrived for the funeral, I couldn't wait to see her. I needed to hug her and tell her I loved her. The first time I saw her, she sobbed uncontrollably and said, "Angie, something's happened to you? You're so different." I had changed a lot and was so thankful that she sensed the love, compassion and gentleness I now felt towards her.

After her brother's funeral, Maysie decided to move back to South Africa as she missed her family deeply. Just over a year later, she came to visit me at my office. I thank God for the wonderful opportunity that unplanned visit gave me to spend some real quality time with her. This was clearly not a case of practising 'forgiveness'. Now, I was able to see through the label of 'gay' to her heart just as God saw her. I could now love her unconditionally. This did not mean that I agreed with her lifestyle. It just meant I could bypass all the points on which I differed with her. I could go straight to her beautiful heart and love her as God loved her. It is possible to learn to be able to both agree or disagree with someone and still love that person.

During her visit, she mentioned she had seen the film "The Passion of Christ" the previous Sunday night. It seemed it had had a profound effect on her. As she sat in my office the following Wednesday morning, discussing the film, (which, incidentally, I hadn't seen), she wept as she recounted some of the parts of the film that affected her very deeply. I felt so privileged to be able to chat with her, helping her through many personal relationship issues that now troubled her, having seen the film. After much talking and crying, she asked me to pray with her. She prayed her own spontaneous prayer that morning, asking God to forgive her for her neglect of Him. She also voiced her forgiveness of all those who had hurt her since her childhood and, more especially, since her sexual orientation had become public knowledge.

She ended by re-dedicating her life to Christ. She asked Him to give her purpose and direction. She asked me to let her have one of my Bibles that she had so often paged through as a child. During her many visits with us when she was younger, she would love paging through my older Bible which I had filled with photographs and little notes—this was the one she wanted. I promised her I would look for it. The following Sunday night, I found the Bible and called her. She was delighted. Again, she thanked me for me for the special time we'd shared together that Wednesday morning. She ended the conversation by saying, "Angie, I know I made the right decision to come back to South Africa. I've really missed my family." She added, "I'll see you at your office in the morning—have the coffee ready! Love you Angie." Little did I know that would be the last proper conversation I would ever have with my precious niece?

At eleven o'clock that night, I heard movements in the house and saw lights were on. I got out of bed to investigate. My daughter, Angelique, had just put the telephone back on its cradle as I walked through. The expression on her face immediately told me something was very wrong. "Mom" she said, "I didn't want to wake you. Maysie's had a car accident. They think she's broken her leg. Go back to bed, Mom. It's not serious. Family and friends have gone to the hospital with her . . . everything will be okay."

Not convinced, I went back to bed and started to pray for her. I felt very uneasy. Two minutes later, I jumped out of bed knowing in my heart I had to get to her. I got dressed and asked Angelique to take me to the hospital.

As we reached the hospital, we were startled to see a friend of Maysie's coming out of the entrance to the emergency rooms screaming, "No! No!" Fear gripped my heart. I summoned the courage to ask, "Where is she?" "They've lost her" the friend blurted out, "She's gone, she's dead". Sobbing, I collapsed to the sidewalk next to the entrance. I begged God to help me in this seemingly hopeless situation. I wailed out to Him,

"Lord, not this way! I so wanted to see her and pray with her and say 'goodbye'. I never knew she was so badly hurt!"

As I sat weeping crumpled on the ground, a nurse came running out, "We've resuscitated her! We have got her back. You can come and see her!" I rushed to her side and held her hand. She was conscious. I asked, if she could hear me, to squeeze my hand. She nodded her head, squeezing my hand so tightly. The emergency staff had inserted a pipe in her mouth, so talking properly was impossible. I asked her if she wanted me to stay with her. She gripped my hand even harder, nodding again. Softly, I prayed with her and assured her I would not leave her alone. She was very scared and shivering with pain. I was so grateful I had decided to come to the hospital.

She was given a number of blood transfusions. She was obviously bleeding internally. When she arrested a second time, we were asked to leave the room. Again, she was brought back from the brink. The attending surgeon told me they were sending her for a scan as they suspected serious internal injuries. We sent for her mother and grandmother who were waiting anxiously at home for news. In my heart, I knew she was very seriously injured. I continued to pray and believe for a miracle.

The surgeon told us that he suspected a ruptured aorta. If that was the case, he said, there would be no more that could be done for her. She was far too unstable to undergo surgery. Her bed was wheeled through to the X-ray Department for the scan. My distraught sister arrived as she was being wheeled back to the room after the scan. The surgeon shook his head, "Her aorta's ruptured. She's only got about 30 minutes to live. I'm so sorry we can't save her." This was the most devastating news for my dear sister to hear. She had lost her eldest son in a car accident a little over a year earlier. Now, she was about to lose her only daughter. She kissed Maysie and collapsed in a heap to the floor wailing. Her husband, her rock and her support, lifted her and, holding her tightly, led her away.

How could this have happened? Was it all real? In the midst of all the anguish and despair, I couldn't begin to imagine the terrible aching grief that lay ahead for my poor sister. To lose two children in such a short space of time was too much to bear.

Back beside the bed, I took her hand and whispered gently to her, "May, May, tonight you are going back to Jesus, my darling girl. You are going to be dancing on streets of gold my, precious child." She understood. Her beautiful blue eyes not leaving mine. She nodded and squeezed my hand. The tears coursed their way down her cheeks. I and all those around the bed, including the nurses, were weeping too. The nurses were so gentle and compassionate. Feeling our desperation, they were crying out, "Jesus, Jesus! This beautiful girl and her family need you. Please help them!" I held her and kissed her. I told her how precious she was to us all . . . how we loved her so much. I stand in awe at the way God had, in His faithfulness, had other Christian believers at her bedside praying for her and supporting us as a family at this critical time. His peace, mercy and grace were so evident at this most important time of her life.

She was slipping away fast. Her grip on my hand, which had been so firm, began to slacken. My darling mother arrived just as she took her last breath. Mum clung to her and whispered, "Goodbye, Mammy Boo. Your Mama loves you so much." Mum had given her that pet name when she was a little girl of three. Maysie had heard the song 'Mammy Blue' and was always singing. In her childish way, she had mistaken 'Blue' for 'Boo'.

It was six in the morning, when I finally let go of that precious hand and kissed her goodbye for the last time. God had been faithful to both of us by letting us have those extra hours together a few days earlier. He had allowed me to pray with her and say goodbye. She died knowing she was so loved by both God and her family and friends. My greatest consolation was that we had absolute assurance that she had returned to her Heavenly home, to the God of her youth.

I am so grateful to have learned to love others, just as God loves us all, unconditionally. Today, I am able see through all the labels society gives people, without judging them . . . just as our Heavenly Father does. What an awesome privilege for me!

Chapter 10 ═══════════════════

A NEW BEGINNING
IN A NEW COUNTRY

After losing my husband, I had no choice but to carry on running the factory and survive as best I could. After all our years of marriage, I was completely unprepared for the trauma of suddenly being on my own. I felt totally ill-equipped to take on the role of being the strong one, holding everything together in both the family and the business.

One morning, some months into this stressful time of transition, I was visiting a friend who mentioned a neighbour of hers who did care-giving overseas a few months each year. Suddenly, she said, "Angela! You'd make a brilliant carer. The children can run the business. You can go and find yourself again. You've all the qualities needed. Why don't you seriously consider it?" Little did I know then what a great impact this visit would have in changing my life. There and then, my friend got up and gave me the Agency's telephone number.

As I drove home, I was filled with a sense of hope and excitement I hadn't experienced in years but confidence, I'm sad to say, was in short supply. I struggled with an avalanche of thoughts about how I would broach the subject with my children and my elderly mother. They would surely think I had gone crazy!

I had to think through all the implications very carefully. We were all very close . . . how would we survive the months of separation? I was the strong one. The whole family relied on me. The thought, "I hate being the strong one!" exploded upon me. All I longed for was to just be me. There were so many reasons why I couldn't possibly be a Carer. I began mulling them over . . . one by one.

Firstly, I had the weighty responsibility of the factory and then there were my family and friends to consider. When it came to the actual job of caring, I was plagued with the thought that the people could very well not like me. Would I be able to I manage all the demands of the job? Where would I even begin? My confidence struck an all-time low.

It crept into my consciousness that my faith had been my anchor all through the many trials in my life. It was the only reason I had survived. I prayed for wisdom. I needed knowledge and guidance. I decided to live one day at a time. If I was to fulfil my heart's desire to be a carer, I had to trust God.

My Mum had always said, "Angie, you can only do your best. Let God do the rest." She was right. I phoned the Agency and then registered for First Aid courses needed as a foundation for the Advanced Home Caring course. Throughout that time of study, my children boosted my ego, telling me how proud they were of me doing this at my age. It was not easy to take on the load of studying, doing assignments and sitting exams at sixty years of age. I applied myself to the task with gusto and diligence. I got the highest marks in the class for the final exam! Perhaps I over-compensated because of my age? To be absolutely honest, it wasn't just that . . . I was terrified of failing and having all the much younger students see me fail . . . a bit of false pride in my character still needing to go?

Having overcome the hurdle of getting suitable qualifications, I now felt equipped. I was now decidedly more confident to take the next step towards becoming a carer. I arranged with the Agency's representative to meet for an interview. I felt very comfortable chatting to her during the two hours it lasted. She assured me I was perfectly suited for the job and encouraged me to pursue it. All the while, I was still working at the factory as normal.

My father had left me a precious heritage in the way of British citizenship. Now, I remembered the many heated arguments I'd had with him over the years about my needing a British passport. He insisted I keep my British Citizenship. I am so grateful he won that particular argument! I was free to live and work in England.

A few months later, the Agency's representative phoned me to say they had the Police Clearances and would love to have me as a carer. When she asked when I would be able to start work, I told her I would have to get back to her. I hadn't given it a thought. It wasn't until later that I realised how perfect her timing had been. Shortly after that call, our main customer cancelled their orders, leaving me no option but to close the factory. I was devastated. We had lost everything! Thank God I had done the First-Aid and home caring courses. Little did I realise just how soon I would be needing those diplomas!

This was a time of hopelessness for the family and the staff at the factory. Mum was so wise during this trying period. I would always feel so uplifted after spending time with her. She encouraged me to book my air ticket and start my caring as soon as possible.

At my age, it would have been impossible to get a job in South Africa. I phoned my cousins in England. I needed a base to stay between assignments and knew that they would provide a safe haven. I could hardly believe my ears when Katie asked me, "Where will you be working from, Angela?" When I replied "Horsham" she burst out laughing, "That's where we've moved to!"

And so began my trip from South Africa to England. Until the last minute, my children had been telling everyone "Our mother will never be able to leave the family . . . we'll believe it when we see it."

How wrong they were! I left South Africa in mid-summer. I spent more time crying in the toilet of the aircraft than in my seat. The prospect of not seeing my family for three months was daunting. I had never been apart from them for this long. The flight seemed endless. I felt so alone. My dearest mother felt my parting the most deeply. We had always had such a close relationship. It really grieved me to leave them all so heartbroken.

I stepped onto English soil early on a grey morning when the mercury hovered around minus nine degrees. My cousin Jonathan and his eldest daughter were at Heathrow to meet me. I was about to begin a new life in England.

Once in Horsham, I was phoned by the Agency to say I needed to go for another interview. After a taxing two hour interview, I was appointed a Co-ordinator. I was to keep in touch with the Agency so I could be allocated my assignments. My cash flow position was somewhat less than favourable and I could hardly afford to mark time not working . . . but I had no choice.

Anxiously, I waited for ten days before I was given my first job. The assignment took me to a little bungalow in a circular road. That first very chilly morning with the thermometer reading two degrees, I was met by the then carer. I was introduced to Bertha, a retired schoolteacher. She was a dear lady, suffering from severe dementia, and lived alone in her home.

I have never before come across such energy in an 88 year old person. She could walk faster than I could run! I was mortified that I was so unfit . . . and so began my walking days. With her English love of walking, Bertha taught me to really walk. In South Africa, the ever-present danger of crime put walking on one's own out of the question. For the first two days, my legs ached unbearably. We covered an average of two to three miles daily. For Bertha, it was a piece of cake. For me, it was agony from start to finish. In time, I got into a walking routine and really enjoyed our many walks and talks together. I am extremely grateful to Bertha for having encouraged me to walk. It was a milestone in my life.

My fitness level rose and I felt very healthy. Bertha was a woman of great intelligence and had a phenomenal long-term memory. I had never encountered the care of people with dementia or Alzheimer's, and so the lessons were about to begin.

My afternoons were spent raptly listening to her great fund of stories of British history in general and Bertha's wartime experiences in particular. I learned so much from her. She had a great skill in filling her tales with so much fascinating detail. I found myself catching up on the history lessons I'd loathed so much as a child.

So often, Bertha would break into song. I was amazed how she remembered every words of the songs. I had never heard most of what she sang. The one I particularly remember was called "Run, Rabbit, Run". When I asked her what it was all about, she very patiently told me, "We had no food in those war days, Angela. We had to catch rabbits so we could eat . . . so the song was telling the rabbits to run away." Her favourite was Vera Lynne's "We'll meet again." I was going to get to know this song very well by the time my days with Bertha were over. Another of her favourites was "A Nightingale sang in Berkley Square" and she always performed a little solo dance in the middle of the sitting room as she sang it. Clearly this dear lady was in another world and another time hugging herself as she danced and sang, the broadest of smiles on her face.

The first night with Bertha, I settled her in bed at about 9.30pm. Around midnight, I was awoken by the sound of running water. I found Bertha showering and washing her hair. When I entered the bathroom, she greeted me, "Good morning, dear!" It was quite a challenge to convince her it was midnight! After I had helped her out the shower and dried her hair, I put her back into bed and went back to bed myself.

Not an hour later, I awoke with a start! Bertha, fully dressed, was standing next to my bed. She announced she was ready for a shopping trip to the local supermarket. It was minus five degrees outside and the snow a good few inches deep. It took some doing to convince her again that it was still very early in the morning and that she still had several hours of sleep.

I was exhausted when I collapsed into bed at 1.45am. Barely an hour later, I woke with a start, aware of someone in my bedroom. It was a replay of what had happened a mere two hours earlier. This time, she announced she was ready for Church. Again, I hauled myself out of bed. Showing her the clock, I gently explained it was still night-time. Very flustered, Bertha apologised and went back to bed for the third time since midnight. Surely, by now she must have been exhausted? Oh no, she certainly wasn't! At 4am, I was awakened to the sound of the television blaring through the house. It can be imagined that was the end of my night's sleep. It was also the first of many nights when my sleep was to be disrupted by dear, sweet Bertha.

When I first started looking after Bertha, she kept herself busy knitting squares which we would sew together to make blankets. Most times, she would knit quietly but, every now and again, she would put the knitting down and tell me she needed to talk to me. "Angela," she would say, "knit, knit, knit. 1 don't like knitting! I don't want to knit anymore! Anyway, what are we knitting these stupid squares for?"

I would patiently explain, "Bertha, the blanket is for Agnes' birthday in October. She has been so kind to you. She needs it for the winter so we must finish it soon." I would change the subject, offering her a cup of tea. "Yes, let's have cup of tea" she would say. No sooner was she seated with her cup of tea than she would say, "I'd better get on with my knitting . . . I love knitting."

When I had started looking after Bertha, I had been given strict instructions: 'No Sugar'. One morning, while we were shopping for milk, I saw her picking up a few chocolates. I quietly went over to her and asked if she wanted to buy the chocolates as a gift for someone. "No," she answered, "they're for me, Angela. I can have chocolates if I feel like them. I love chocolates!" I gently reminded her she had a problem with sugar and wasn't allowed any sweets. That was not a wise thing to have said! Hands on her hips, she turned to me, "Angela, I'm 89 years old! I should know whether I am allowed to eat chocolates or not. I've eaten them all my life." I answered as calmly as I could, "Okay, Bertha. Let's pay the lady for the chocolates." Turning around, she went back to the shelf, "I'll put them back." The shopkeeper smiled and winked at me. Everybody knew Bertha well . . . she was a long-time resident of the area.

I grew to be very fond of Bertha. She will always be one of my favourites. She was my very first client, certainly a very draining one emotionally, physically and mentally at times, but I soon learned how to snatch times of rest when I could, as one does with a new baby. I enjoyed my stay with her very much but, all too soon, my assignment with Bertha was over. By then, I certainly had grown in confidence. I had done it! I was now a carer.

I returned to look after dear Bertha many times until she got too frail to live in her own home. She is now well cared for in a nursing home. I stay in contact with her family, phoning or texting regularly to see how Bertha is. Although the Alzheimer's has locked her into her own little world, she is happy and at peace with herself.

Chapter 11

THE MAD ENGLISHMAN AND HIS CAT

By the end of my first assignment, I had grown very fond of Bertha. I was extremely grateful for having had the opportunity of working for such a kind, respectful and most appreciative family in my first caring job.

After a few days break, I launched into my next assignment, this time in a very affluent part of rural England. It didn't take long for me to discover that not all my clients would be like dear Bertha and her lovely family.

My clients, Edward and his wife Nancy, had just celebrated their 40th wedding anniversary. Sadly, they both had cancer and the husband had also suffered a stroke. I had been told by the Agency that the couple had a cat which I might have to feed. I was happy to do that. I hadn't envisaged that 'cat carer' would be part of my job description!

Shortly after my arrival, I was introduced to Foofie, their white, blind, deaf and grossly overweight Persian cat. She was obviously the Queen of this home. She had the most beautiful basket which I came to call 'Foofie's Throne'. It was extremely ornate and made of genuine leather and fur, which had to be brushed and aired daily. Furnished with a soft woollen blanket and her toys, her 'throne' sat in the corner of the kitchen, elevated on a special table with two little steps leading up to her 'boudoir'.

My clients clearly doted on Queen Foofie. However, I was horrified at the appalling manner in which he spoke to and treated his wife. It amazed me how this couple, and particularly Nancy, kept up a non-stop barrage of talk at the deaf cat. Foofie would stumble into the walls and furniture with Nancy running after her, trying to encourage her to change directions. Edward would be hot on her heals, screeching at the top of his voice, "Nancy! Leave the cat alone! She needs to work things out for herself. She'll soon learn after she's walked into a few walls." Crying, the miserable Nancy would hobble back to her chair at the kitchen table. From the time they got up through to bedtime, this was the style of their day.

Edward was forever intimidating his poor wife in front of me. I was deeply saddened by his unkind attitude to his poor wife. Mealtimes were an absolute nightmare. He would keep up a steady flow of nasty comments, passing rude remarks about what she did or didn't eat. If she left anything on her plate, he would blast her with a five minute lecture after the meal. Her every word was criticised or contradicted by him. I found his unbelievable rudeness extremely embarrassing and wondered how Nancy had put up with it and his interfering ways all those years.

As a widow, it hurt me deeply to see a married couple locked in such an ugly, abusive situation. Given the seriousness of their illnesses, they had no guarantee of years of life ahead. The couple had lived a privileged life in some Eastern country for many years with retinues of servants. To them, a care-giver was just another servant. I wasn't bothered by the domestic chores. Ironically, Edward was always impeccably polite to me and appallingly rude to his own wife.

One exceptionally chilly day (minus 2degrees), I had to take Foofie to the vacant greenhouse to do her toileting. "What a privileged feline to have her very own private cat-carer to take her to the toilet!" What would my children think of that? Their mother who had never had to make a bed, empty a bin or wash and iron clothes had now become a toilet assistant to a cat!

I was yet to discover some of Edward's very strange habits and the rules he had imposed with regards to certain issues in the home. He had dictated that only one bin bag was to be used a week in the large stainless steel kitchen bin. I was informed that they were very expensive. This meant a disgusting ritual was played out every day. When Edward disappeared into his study, Nancy would start delving through the bin, digging out the rubbish and decanting it into smaller bags. These I had to deposit in the larger outside bin when her husband was not around. I was told to be careful that he didn't see me going to the bin. I was flabbergasted at these people!

Because Edward insisted that washing wore clothes out and that their water and gas bills were too high, they only did their laundry once a week They were extremely wealthy with their designer clothes, their opulent home and lavish meals, the best cars and expensive horses and even their own airplane. Despite their obvious wealth, they had some very strange ideas about saving money . . . 'straining gnats and swallowing big fat camels'.

This very disturbing situation called for a lot of thought and prayer. It was beyond belief that people could live like this. After a few days with them, I was phoned by the Agency. I was asked whether I would stay a further two weeks as the couple really liked me. I told my co-ordinator I didn't think I could stay the extra time. I found the situation too upsetting. It was an awful atmosphere to live and work in. I never knew when Edward might fly into a rage with his wife. I was continually on my guard, waiting for 'Mount Edward' to erupt and spew his abuse at Nancy. My heart was so sore for her.

My co-ordinator was very understanding. She explained how it was very difficult placing carers in Edward and Nancy's home. After their first experience, none of them would stay on or consider a second round. She asked me if I was having my two hour compulsory break during the day. I wasn't. I was at their beck and call from 7am to 10pm. The only times I sat were mealtimes. She challenged me to speak up. I had never been a confrontational person so I found this advice very difficult to follow. Without my knowing, she telephoned the couple's daughter to tell her what was happening.

That evening, while Edward was watching television, Nancy called me to the bedroom. She told me Margaret their daughter had phoned and had been very angry with Edward. She begged me to please stay on. Margaret had told Edward that, if I left, there would be no more carers and she would put them in a private nursing home. As all the carers had complained about his behaviour, the Agency felt it unfair to send any more carers into this hostile environment. I ached for Nancy and told her I would think about it and give her my answer in the morning.

The next day was shopping day. I had to drive and accompany Edward to the supermarket. Before we left, Nancy called me to one side, asking me to get her a bag of hot chips at the local fish and chips store. Being so ill, there were days when she had no appetite at all. She was so thin and so I was happy to be able to get her something she would enjoy. We hadn't realised that Edward had overheard her asking me. It was as though World War 3 had begun. He shouted and screamed in a maniacal way at poor, cowering Nancy. I grabbed my purse and hurried to the car as fast as I could and waited for him.

After some time, Edward got into the car. He said he needed to talk to me before we left for the shops. I mentally braced myself, "Here it comes!" He asked me if I was happy working for them. Steeling myself, I told him, "Not at all." Unperturbed, he inquired if I felt I had too much work. Before I could answer, he apologised for not having given me my two hour break every day. He assured me he would make them up in whatever way it suited me. I replied that I did need my breaks. More importantly, I said I was extremely offended and grieved by the way he spoke to his wife in front of me. I was getting bolder by the moment as I laid it on the line that I found him very disrespectful, unloving and unkind to her. I went on, "Edward, I am recently widowed. I know how short life can be. I would give anything to spend five minutes with my late husband but that's a chapter that's closed for me. It's not too late for you and Nancy. You are so fortunate to still have each other. You still have time to enjoy and love each other. Please don't waste the precious time you have left." I couldn't believe how brave I had been. I was very apprehensive about the response I was about to get to my bold retort and mini-lecture. Edward asked me to give him an example of what he was doing or saying that was so offensive. I obliged, mentioning the recent episode when Nancy asked me to buy her chips. I went on to catalogue his constant screaming at and belittling of Nancy in front of me. I described how I loathed mealtimes because of the screaming matches with her. I mentioned how she found refuge in loving her cat and finding great comfort in holding Foofie and her assiduous efforts to prevent Foofie from hurting herself. I found it strange that he never showed his wife any affection or kindness. He listened intently. After about a minute of pondering what I had said, he said, "You are right. You are quite right, my girl. Thank you for having the courage to tell me the truth about myself. No-one else has ever bothered to do so. I've just been left to be the horrible old man that I am. I am very sorry indeed for my bad behaviour. Will you give me a second chance?" I was stunned at his reaction. I agreed . . . it was wonderful to see the decision to change his attitude to his long-suffering wife. The cathartic experience of having confronted this man in an honest and unemotional way did much for my confidence.

From then on, every time we went out, Edward would ask his wife, "Nancy, is there anything you would like us to get you while we are out?" The radical change in the old man in was remarkable. Nancy began to smile more and I never saw her cower or cry again. One day, on one of our shopping trips, he exclaimed, "Oh dear! I forgot to ask Nancy if she needed anything! Can you suggest something she might like?" I suggested a bunch of fresh flowers. We chose them together. Nancy was overjoyed with the flowers and kept returning to the vase to smell and admire the flowers over the next few days. As a modern-day Cupid, I pushed their chairs closer together in the TV Lounge. It was wonderful to see them interacting as loving spouses should. I even saw him gently stroking her hand one evening. By the time with them came to an end, the transformation in their relationship had been profound. I was really glad I had relented and stayed even when the going got to be so tough.

My three months of caring was up. I was due to fly back to South Africa to my beloved family. With an overloaded case and a happy heart, I boarded the plane for home thinking, "Angela, you did it! You are an experienced care-giver now . . . and the best cat-carer out! You survived that mad Englishman and his cat!"

Chapter 12 _____

THE PERFECT GENTLEMAN

It had been a year I had been doing the caring work in England by the time I returned to South Africa for Christmas. After I had got home, the Agency called me to offer me the assignment of caring for a gentleman. Initially, I was extremely hesitant. I replied I would confirm whether I would accept it within an hour.

I voiced my fears and lack of confidence about caring for a man to Mum. I felt particularly apprehensive as the job involved personal care. Mum laughed, "Angela, this is a challenge! You must be able to cope with all aspects of caring and men are a part of the challenge. Pretend you are washing a child. Just chat away and, before you know it, it will be over. When you've done it once, it won't bother you again." I called the agency and accepted the assignment to care for a blind, retired farmer in the countryside in Kent.

It was minus nine degrees when I arrived in England at the end of December . . . a vast contrast to the African sunshine I had just been enjoying. As I waited for my luggage at the carousel at Heathrow that early morning, I switched on my mobile phone. There was a message from the Agency, asking me to do an emergency five day assignment before starting with the farmer. I was to start the next day, looking after a 99 year old lady. Her permanent care-giver was laid up for five days with a bad back. In hindsight, that piece of information should have set the warning bells ringing. I decided to accept. I reasoned it would

106

prove most interesting to meet such a grand old lady. I had never met anyone that age in my life.

I arrived the next morning at the address I had been given and was introduced to Anna by Sophia, her care-giver, who was obviously in great pain. After a quick handover, Sophia left to return to her apartment upstairs. Mentally, my charge was as sharp as a pin. She was very tall and extremely frail, not able to walk at all. Although she was a lovely soul, she was my most challenging assignment to date. Without any mechanical aids to help me, caring for her involved much lifting and physical strain on my back. Having undergone a spinal fusion myself, I should have avoided falling into this trap. Although Anna was not really overweight, it was very difficult to move or lift her. She could not help me at all or co-operate by moving her legs. The Agency had specifically instructed me that lifting a patient was not permitted but, sometimes, in a crisis situation, certain things just have to be done.

Every night, at about 9.30, I would literally crawl upstairs to my bedroom and lean against the radiator to ease the terrible pain in my back. I would no sooner have settled down to sleep when the bell would ring. How I hated that bell ringing at night! Anna refused to wear the correct underwear for her incontinence. This inevitably resulted in having to change her nightdress and bed linen up to three times a night, not to mention all the clothing changes during the day. I had never seen so much dirty laundry in all my life. That too was my department. I couldn't see how I would ever get through this assignment. It was proving incredibly strenuous and demanding. During the first night I was there, the snow began to fall and didn't stop for the next five days. On the last day, I thanked God for the strength and ability I had been given to get through that difficult period. I was so grateful my time here would soon come to an end and I would be off to take up my assignment with the blind farmer. I phoned the taxi service to confirm their arrival time the next day. To my horror, I was told that the roads were far too dangerous because of the heavy snowfalls. The taxi service wouldn't be operating for at least 48 hours. I couldn't imagine how I would ever survive two more days and nights of this torture. Anna was delighted to have me for the extra time!

The final night was the most difficult of all. Anna rang her bell four times between 10pm and 5am. She had to be washed and the bed linen changed three times. I was mentally and physically exhausted. I was also suffering from sleep deprivation as I hadn't more than three hours sleep any of the nights I had been with this 99 year old. I crawled up to my room the next morning, the 7th of January, at 5am. I begged God to help me. I once again called the taxi service, hoping the state of the roads had improved. The answer was that they were not operating until the next day . . . weather permitting. Anna asked if I could cancel my other assignment. She wanted me to stay a further two weeks with her. My heart sank. I quickly replied, "I'm sorry. I have made a commitment to the farmer who is expecting me. I must get to him as soon as the roads are safe to travel."

I was so engrossed in the enormous load of laundry that morning, that I nearly didn't hear the taxi service ringing to tell me they were outside the front door waiting for me. I couldn't believe my ears! I rushed to the door to check and sure enough the taxi was really there. I asked the driver to wait while I fetched my case and said my goodbyes.

I sprinted upstairs as fast as I could. My bags had been packed in anticipation of a swift departure. I pulled on my shoes and coat and went to the care-giver's apartment to tell her I was leaving. From the look on her face, it was very plain she was not at all pleased. I felt no guilt as I had helped her out with the extra time. She looked well enough to return to work. I said goodbye to Anna and got into the taxi with a sigh of relief. That was the toughest assignment I ever took on. No amount of compassion or money was worth the stress and strain involved. Anna needed two people to care for her . . . one for the day and the other for the night. It was little wonder Sophia had a back problem!

The taxi wound its way slowly around the icy and highly dangerous bends in the roads bends. By this time, my exhaustion level had so outweighed my fear of those icy roads . . . I was happily prepared to take the risk and move on to the farmer's house. It had to be an improvement on what I had just left.

The snow was about a foot deep when I arrived at the large white farmhouse. I plodded my way to the front door in my ordinary summer shoes I was wearing when I had left Anna in such a rush. The snow coming halfway up my calves. I rang the doorbell. I was greeted by a lovely girl who had booked the same taxi to go back into town. She did a speedy handover in the cosy kitchen, introducing me to Leo, a short man sitting in a chair. His eyes closed, he offered me his hand in greeting. I introduced myself and we chatted for a while.

After we had had lunch together, I went upstairs to unpack, having a quick look at the rooms on my way. The house had been built around 1858. The rooms were old fashioned and in dire need of a woman's touch. During one of our many chats in the days which lay ahead, I asked Leo if I could write a chapter about him in this book. He replied, "I will be honoured if you include me in your book." When I first penned these lines, I was still with Leo and had the privilege of reading this chapter to him.

The first night after dinner, I had to help him undress and get him into bed for the night. Leo was an absolute gentleman. I felt quite safe and comfortable with him. Because of his being blind and unable to get up during the night without my assistance, he had to use urine bottles during the night. Having been a farmer all his life, he spoke about everything in very matter-of-fact agricultural terms. I was sitting at the breakfast table breakfast one morning when he said to me, "Angela, you are not a big feeder. You are not eating enough." I was taken aback, "How do you know what I'm eating? You can't see." His immediate reply was, "I can hear you." He never missed a thing. When I was preparing vegetables or cooking, he could tell me exactly what I was doing. He had been blind for some twelve years but he knew exactly what was happening around him all the time.

Extremely disciplined about exercise and a keeping healthy lifestyle, Leo walked around the courtyard every morning and afternoon. He was very knowledgeable on a wide range of subjects. I enjoyed talking to him as we walked around for 15 to 20 minutes every day. He would go out on his usual walking-frame and change to his four-wheeled exercise one in the courtyard so he could walk quicker. When he wanted me to change frames, he would say. "It's time to change horses, Angela". I found his all his idiosyncrasies so amusing. He may have been blind but he was certainly one of the brightest, most positive, cheerful people I have ever had the pleasure of meeting.

Leo never wore pyjama trousers to at night as he had to use urine bottles through the night. Each evening, I would go in at 8 o'clock to give him his final medications for the night. One evening, he was sitting on the edge of the bed as I put each tablet into his mouth. After each one, he sipped his water. Just as I was about to put the last one in his mouth, I dropped it. It fell right into his pubic hair area! "Is that the lot?" he said. Very flustered, I answered, "I'm afraid I've dropped the last tablet", desperately trying not to giggle. I have always laughed easily and found it very hard to smother my giggles. "Well, can you see where it's fallen?" he asked. "No, I can't." I lied reluctantly. There was no way I was going to rescue that tablet from where it had fallen. "Oh, don't worry," he said, "It's only one tablet." I was so relieved he couldn't see my face just then. I helped him settle in his bed and then rushed out of the room, my hand clamped over my mouth, hoping he wouldn't hear my muffled laughter. I summoned the courage to tell Leo the acutely embarrassing story many months later. He almost laughed his head off! My mother could scarcely stop laughing when I told her the story. She knew very well what a prude I was.

Leo loved entertaining and there was an endless stream of visitors for meals at the farm and guests being taken for lunches to the local pub. His knowledge of the local area and memories of people and events in general was amazing. People loved him and his stories about his early years, particularly the ones involving the history of the area where he had lived for 87 years. As a younger man, he had been a keen horseman and I enjoyed hearing about the various celebrities who had been part of the hunts he organised. He still allowed his property to be used for the hunting. It was beautiful to see the horses galloping across the farmlands, their riders kitted in their smart red and black attire. Leo had a fund of fascinating tales to tell about the famous people and politicians lived in the area.

One day, I noticed on a windowsill a photograph of a very regal-looking woman in Victorian dress on a white horse. I thought it might have been one of Leo's ancestors. "Oh no, Angela, that's Raquel Welsh, the film star, on my horse during the filming of 'Elizabeth the First' many years ago."

The old farmer was an ardent fan of Winston Churchill who had grown up in the nearby town. My father had also been a great admirer of Britain's war-time leader and so I enjoyed hearing Leo's stories about him,

Being blind, Leo was avid listener to talking-books and his knowledge on different subjects astounded me. At 87 years of age, he was still ready to absorb new information, keeping up-to-date with the latest technology and with World news.

As time passed, Leo became incapable of taking his walks on his own. His co-ordination and sense of direction deteriorated sharply and he had to be accompanied everywhere. I have never seen anyone his age so determined to get their daily exercise. He would have put many people years his junior to shame.

He had a great sense of humour and we enjoyed many laughs together. It was so wonderful to see him chuckling, his hunched shoulders bobbing up and down as he laughed.

The farm cattle would come right up to the fence around the car park when Leo took his walks. It was as though they'd especially come to greet him. They remained on watch throughout the duration of his walk, slowly chewing the cud. They would look up occasionally with their sad, droopy brown eyes framed by their long lashes, blinking and staring at us for our whole walk. These daily turns around the yard turned into agricultural lessons. I became quite knowledgeable about cows, their habits, breeding, feeding and milking.

Looking back over my years as a carer, I know I have been very blessed to have had such special clients to look after. Since remarrying, I cannot take on long assignments anymore, but I will continue to look after my old farmer Leo for as long as I can. Sadly, my little lady Edwina from Dorset passed away recently, so Leo will be seeing me for as long as he needs me. Apart from him, though, I will work for shorter periods nearer my home near Manchester.

I am often asked when I will stop doing care work, as though it's too much for me physically at my age. I love the old folk I care for. To have the privilege of seeing them entertaining their family and friends in an independent, dignified way and helping them to live in and enjoy their own homes is such a deep pleasure. I have told my children that the day that I can no longer care for these people as I would do for my own parents will be when I stop doing the caring work. Until then, God willing, I will help them enjoy a few more years of quality living.

Chapter 13

GOODBYE MUM

It was the morning of the 27th January 2010. For the previous two days, I had been deep in troubled thought about my son Stephen and his history of addiction. He had been missing for four days. Having never suffered from depression, I presumed my uneasy feeling was due to Stephen's disappearance.

The day started as usual. I was up at six o'clock, dressed and ready to start the day with my wonderful old gentleman farmer Leo. I was really enjoying this assignment. I had never cared for a man before and had been pleasantly surprised at how accommodating this dear old man was.

The morning progressed as normal until, at about 10am, my mother phoned from South Africa. Oh, how I missed her ready smile and the wonderful chats we so often had enjoyed in her bedroom before my return to England a month earlier. Mum was crying. She seldom cried or complained, no matter how difficult things might have been. I knew she had been feeling very poorly and she said she was experiencing the worst pain she had ever endured in her life. No medication was having any effect. "Please, Angie, pray for me, my girl," she pleaded. I felt so utterly helpless but prayed with her. We chatted a little while longer. Then she said she was tired and needed to try and have a nap.

I felt a deep sadness in my heart. I continued praying for her the whole day, trusting she would soon be better. Late that afternoon, Mum phoned again, sounding more cheerful. "I've got your little granddaughter Faith with me and she's just taken her first steps in front of me! I had to tell you!" She was delighted. Mum adored children and this had made her day. We spoke a while longer. She told me she was feeling a little better and had had quite a few visitors that afternoon while she'd been resting. She had got up for an hour and played games with my sisters, something she loved to do. We said our goodbyes. I was relieved she had sounded so much better.

It was just two hours later that the phone rang. My brother Derrick, struggling to talk, said, "Angie, I wish I was there with you, Sis. I've got some bad news." "Is it Stephen?" I fearfully asked. "No, it's Mom. We've lost her. She's gone." Collapsing onto the nearby chair, I felt as though I had been punched in the stomach. I was devastated. I felt I had let my precious mother down being so far away when she needed me the most.

I had to get back to South Africa as soon as possible. My children would be needing me as much as I desperately needed them in this time of shock and sadness. How had she died so suddenly? I knew she had been diagnosed with another aneurysm in October, but Mum had always been so strong that I had believed in my heart she would be with us for a few more years. I mulled over how our family would survive without Mum's unconditional love and support. She had been the heart of our family, our mentor, our advisor, our peacekeeper. She had been the one person who always there for everyone in any kind of need, with the right words and answers for everything . . . and now she was gone. I questioned how I would personally live without her. Oh, how I cried to the Lord that night! My emotions tumbled over each other . . . I was happy for Mum . . . she was no longer in pain . . . at last, she was with her Lord and Saviour she loved so much. I knew I was being selfish and feeling sorry for myself wishing she could have stayed longer, but it was impossible! My beloved mother had gone. I had to accept the reality of that. I had to honour her by coping as best I could.

I took something to help me sleep before I climbed into bed. I felt numb. Would I wake up the next morning, and find it had all just been an awful dream? I started packing as I knew I would be leaving early in the morning. The sooner I got ready the better. After a long hot bath, I got into bed and cried myself to sleep.

My youngest sister phoned me very early the next morning to say she had booked my flight from London at six that evening. I'm so thankful she had done that. It was one less thing for me to worry about. The farmer's neighbour very kindly drove me through to my cousins in Horsham who took me to the airport.

As I walked through passport control and made my way to the boarding gates, my thoughts were constantly on Mum. How was I ever going to carry on without her? Would I ever be happy again? I walked down the familiar passage I had walked down so many times before when returning to South Africa. I remembered my last trip home. I had planned to go in December but, because Mum had been in and out of hospital twice since I had last been to Durban, I had thought perhaps I should go back return earlier to celebrate her birthday with her. That thought had kept coming back to me. I had decided to change my ticket and go home earlier. Little did I realise that the Lord was preparing me for the next step along the road of crucial change in my life. He knew He was going to call my very special Mum home just two months later. By going home earlier, I was blessed with having a really special time with her. The memories of that will remain with me forever. I was so glad I had obeyed the gentle prompting from the Lord and invested that invaluable, precious time with my darling mother and spent her last birthday and Christmas with her.

I shall never forget Mum's excitement the day I arrived at her home. My son-in-law Marc went into the house and told her he had bought a plant for her birthday. He asked if she would come out into the garden to show him where she would like it planted. As she walked out of the front door, she saw me walking up the stairs. She jumped up and down like a little child, clapping, crying and laughing all at the same time. She was so tiny, only 4ft 10inches tall. "Have I died and gone to heaven? Is that really you, my Angie?" At the time, I had no idea how prophetic those words were prove to be very shortly after this visit. Now, here I was going back to South Africa, but that beautiful, smiling face would never greet me again. Before I had left for England the first time, I had been living with Mum. We used to do so much together. I treasure the very special memories of that wonderful season in our two lives.

The church was filled to capacity for my dear Mum's funeral. The dignified order of service was a fitting memorial to my wonderful mother. Mum and Dad had jokingly been referred to each other as the British Bulldog and his little French Poodle throughout their lives. Dad was the tough one and Mum always the gentle, gracious lady. In the eulogy, my daughter Angelique mentioned the little French Poodle once again walking alongside her British Bulldog. The congregation laughed and clapped their hands at this.

I know I received the greatest inheritance of all from my mother . . . I had enjoyed 60 years of unconditional love, wisdom, friendship, support, loyalty and guidance from her. The legacy of this would now carry me to the end of my earthly life till Mum and I meet again in our heavenly home. As I honoured her in life, I will honour her in death. There would be life after Mum!

IT'S NEVER TOO LATE
TO FACE YOUR FEAR

I had been in Dorchester, in the county of Dorset for almost two months. The peace and quaintness of that part of England have always captivated and charmed me. I was caring for a true lady called Edwina. She was a widow and extremely particular about every aspect of her lifestyle. I was very grateful for my upbringing. Mum and Dad had the gift of hospitality and were constantly entertaining dignitaries so we learned from an early age to do things the 'proper way'. Table settings, manners and hospitality were very important to Edwina. She was thrilled that I was able to help her entertain her family and friends with excellence. Ever since my arrival at Edwina's, her daughter Judy had made constant reference to "Ruby" and "Kitty" in her conversations with her mother. I assumed they were her friends. However, if they were her friends, I was a little perplexed as to why she spoke so strangely about them. I assumed maybe this was just a quirky 'English' idiosyncrasy and that perhaps I should just mind my own business.

We were having coffee together one afternoon, when Judy again brought up the subject of 'Ruby' with her mother. She mentioned how 'Ruby' had put on so much weight and that she could no longer put on her shoes. This conjured up for me a picture of an alarmingly obese lady who could not bend down to pull her shoes onto her feet. Eventually, my curiosity got the better of me! "Are Ruby and Kitty close friends of yours?" I asked. The two women burst out into gales of laughter! What had I said that was so amusing? Judy cleared up my confusion when she told me that Ruby was a brood mare who had been on her way to the salami factory in Italy when Judy had rescued her. I have had an aversion to salami ever since!

Shortly afterwards, family members visiting Edwina were taken horse-riding by Judy and seemed to thoroughly enjoy their excursion. They were all without any riding experience whatsoever.

I remembered the last horse ride I'd had many years before when I had been all of 12 years old. A birthday party was being held at our family home with many friends and family celebrating with us. Mum and Dad's friend, Muriel, had brought horses to give the children rides. I recalled how it was my turn to climb onto the horse's back. I had 'thought' I could ride alone. I was thoroughly enjoying my ride when, suddenly, my delight turned to horror! I will never know what caused the horse to panic. It started rearing and bucking, neighing wildly. My total lack of experience as a rider showed itself immediately . . . I lost my grip and slid down its back, landing on the driveway with a mighty thump! I was very shaken and covered with acute embarrassment.

My Grandfather, Papa, rushed to help me up. After checking I was not hurt, he did everything in his power to coax me back onto the horse again. Even today, I can clearly hear him firmly saying, "Angela, you must get back on this horse, my girl. If you don't, you will always be scared of horses. Please, my girl, listen to your Papa". He had been a keen horseman for many years and obviously knew what he was talking about. Nothing and no-one could have persuaded me to get back on that horse. Feeling thoroughly embarrassed, I leapt to my feet, pretending I was absolutely fine. I made a dash to the house and straight to my bedroom to 'lick my wounded pride' and rub my very painful posterior. Papa was right—I never did get back on a horse ever again . . . until one day while I was in Dorchester . . .

I was 62 years old when I decided to conquer that fear of horses which had haunted me all those years. The visitors returned from their equestrian foray with such obvious pleasure on their faces. After having heard their enthusiastic comments after their ride and especially after being told how gentle Ruby was, I decided the day had arrived for me to face my fear. I was going to get back on a horse again. Maybe Ruby was the just the right horse for me to ride? I had a chat to Julia. She was more than delighted to be able to accommodate my request. The date was set for me . . . the following Sunday I would embark upon my famous 'face-my-fear ride'!

The fateful Sunday morning arrived. Judy came to fetch me. I had woken several times during the night gripped by panic, "I don't know if I'm really up to this! What am I trying to prove? What if I take another tumble?" I decided I was just being a coward. I had to do this, even if there would never be a repeat performance!

When it started raining on our drive to the stables, I thought, "This would happen. I'm sure I'm just not meant to do this foolish thing!" I pondered that, if that were the case, the rain would get me out of the jam I found myself in. The rain was no problem to Judy. She stopped off at her house on the way and, after we'd had a cup of tea, kitted me out in riding boots and riding hat while we waited for the rain to stop. I wasn't going to get out of this one easily.

I have found while I have lived in England that the vagaries of the weather do not deter the English from getting on with life . . . whether it's snowing, sleeting, blowing up a storm or just drizzling. The rain soon eased off and we headed to the field where Ruby was grazing. Judy put the reins on her and led her to the gate where I was apprehensively waiting. As I caught sight of the horse, I froze. She seemed to assume the proportions of a descendant of a great heroic mythological steed! I was completely intimidated by the sheer size of the creature. I doubted I'd ever be able to mount her let alone ride her. But Judy had everything organised . . . a red plastic milk crate perched on top of a forty four gallon drum was how I would mount Ruby.

Ruby was saddled-up at the stables and brought to the drum and crate construction where I was already perched. Precariously balanced on the drum as Ruby was positioned alongside, I was seized by the thought "Angela, are you stark raving mad! What are you trying to prove?" I quickly dismissed the thought and clambered onto Ruby. She didn't budge! My immediate reaction was that Fate had decreed that I was not meant to ride this horse! Judy, meanwhile, was urging Ruby to move. I was instructed to kick the horse's sides gently with my boots an make clicking noises with my tongue! I dissolved into giggles. It got worse as the whole scene conjured up for me an episode from the comedy series 'Keeping up Appearances' where the lady of the house resorted to the same clicking routine on her disastrous outing on the back of a horse. I couldn't stop laughing. We were going nowhere very rapidly. I am sure Judy was extremely irritated by it all but she remained very patient and polite.

Judy started pulling Ruby by the lead. I continued the kicking and the clicking. I am so relieved that my children weren't around . . . I must have been quite a sight! In desperation, Judy offered Ruby some hay and carrots. This did the trick and, at last, she decided to move at an excruciatingly slow pace which then picked up to a gentle trot. I couldn't believe it . . . I was actually riding a horse! A miracle indeed! I was beginning to really take to this riding lark and was enjoying the adventure of it all. And then we struck an incline. This clearly didn't appeal to Ruby. She slowed to a virtual halt. The clicking and kicking routine began again. The hill became a little steeper. As we got near the top, my camera fell out of my pocket. Whether the camera hit Ruby on the bottom or whether the noise startled her as it hit the ground, I will never know. She started a violent bucking and I was convinced I was about to fly over her head. Then she reared backwards. I was determined that I was not about to fall off this horse no matter how much she reared and tried to dislodge me. I clung on for dear life with all my strength. Judy's eyes were as huge as saucers. She grabbed the reins at the side of Ruby's head and calmed her down. Off we went again.

I'm convinced Ruby sensed my fear. Judy said she had never done anything like that before. I had certainly had my fill of riding for one day! I had accomplished what I had set out to do after fifty years, I had ridden a horse! Back at the stables, I had to dismount. I had assumed we would be returning to the 'big drum' for this exercise. I was wrong. Judy informed me that was not the way to get off a horse. I had to throw my left leg behind me and slide down Ruby's right side to the ground. My mount was so tall that it seemed I was sliding down the whole length of the Empire State Building! I landed on both feet with a thump. I am positive Ruby was just as relieved as I was that our ride was at last over. Ridiculous as this petty experience may seem, it was a really great achievement for me. My fear had been conquered after fifty long years and I was very proud of myself!

Chapter 15

FINDING LOVE
"THE SECOND TIME" AROUND

I had been doing caring work for three months in England when I returned to South Africa to visit my family.

One evening, my daughter and her husband sat me down as they had decided their mother needed some strong counsel! They told me that the time had come for me to move on with my life: I needed to work less and have more time for myself, to give myself a chance to meet someone—in other words, I needed a gentleman friend! It had been several years since Vernon had died. I was quite content simply to be a mother and grandmother for the rest of my life.

My children kept on nagging me about opening my options to find a mate again. The Sunday evening before I left South Africa to return to the United Kingdom, my son-in-law Marc, tapping away on his computer, exclaimed, "Mom, this sounds just right for you!" I peered over his shoulder at 'Friends First', the Christian website he had opened. As the name implied, it was one that encouraged simple friendships, no strings attached . . .

"Mom, judging by the excellent reviews this site has, I'm sure most people joining would be of a decent calibre. I'm going to upload your profile and photograph. I'm sure you are going to make some great friends!"

A couple of months after my return to the UK, I received a letter from 'Friends First' with profiles of various men attached. I glanced cursorily through them and put them in my drawer.

A few nights later, Lisa phoned. "Mum, have you made any new friends through that website yet?" I told her I'd received the profiles but had not made contact with anyone. After she'd hung up, I took the list of profiles from the drawer and looked through them once again. Something caught my eye. One of the men had been a South African before moving to England. I made the decision that, if I was to make any contact at all, this was going to be the one . . . only because of his South African roots.

The next day, I summoned the courage to dial the number . . . no reply, just an answering service. He was obviously out. Relieved, I told myself that, at least, I could tell Lisa I had tried. I hastily left my name and phone number before replacing the receiver.

The phone rang later that evening. It was him! Frozen where I stood, I felt myself blushing deeply! I was assailed by an avalanche of mixed emotions   here I was talking to 'another man' for the first time since losing my husband.

Owen told me he was a widower. He had also gone through much trauma and had been the victim of crime in South Africa. He had immigrated to England with his family some thirteen years earlier. As our conversation moved along, we found we had a lot in common: we both had boats and caravans back in South Africa; our families both used to go water-skiing on the same dams; we had visited the same resorts and had our caravans parked permanently at the same beach. It was uncanny how, through all the years of living in South Africa, we had never met. Owen also knew some of my business acquaintances.

From that signal day on, Owen called me virtually every day. During one of our conversations, he asked me if I would ever consider marrying again. Until then, I had been quite content and really hadn't even imagined myself with a man other that Vernon. I told Owen that I really couldn't say. I had certain pre-requisites. It would have to be a very special man to meet them. He asked what they were. I detailed the list: the man would have to be a Christian; there would be no intimacy outside of marriage; I would insist on tests for sexually transmitted diseases before marrying and the man would have to be impeccable with his hygiene. For a few moments which lingered liked an eternity, there was silence on the other end of the phone.

I panicked. I had done exactly what Lisa had told me not to do. I'd put him off before even having met him. Owen then answered, "You are quite right." I thought at the time he was probably being polite. He rang off shortly afterwards. "I've blown it!" I thought ruefully. I had been widowed for so long and, before that, there had only ever been one man in my life. I hadn't a clue about dating a man.

I obviously hadn't put him off completely because the next night he called again. Owen sounded a kind person, so I presumed he was just being polite and would put a gradual end to our telephone friendship so as to not to hurt me. I was wrong again! He wanted us to meet. Because of the great distance between our homes, I ventured that we meet halfway. He suggested Oxford. So, Oxford it would be! He offered to book us into a Bed-and-Breakfast. I sharply replied, "That's fine, but please book two rooms in our separate names! Before we embark on this meeting, I want to make it very clear I would like to pay my own way." Owen agreed.

I was a mass of nerves as I waited outside the bus station in Oxford for Owen to arrive. When he appeared, he looked even nicer than he had in his photograph. He was well-groomed and dressed and smelled really good. Clearly he was wearing good cologne, something which really appealed to me. I could feel myself blushing like a young girl. "Oh my goodness, what am I doing, meeting a strange man in a strange town and being impressed by his cologne?" I was completely intimidated by the thought of how this weekend might progress. I had lost all confidence!

Owen was very chatty. That really helped me through the initial attack of nerves. It was one thing talking on the telephone all those months. Meeting him face-to-face was an entirely different ball game. I was quite confident on the other end of the line during our lengthy conversations. Now, I just clammed up.

We booked into the bed-and-breakfast and then went into town. Owen's manners were impeccable. He did all the right things a woman could expect of a gentleman. Gradually, I felt the tension evaporate and I began to relax.

That evening, when he took me out to dinner, he gave me a gift of a lovely, dainty bedside clock in a pink leather case. The card with it read simply, "After all this time, we meet—Owen." It was such an appropriate gift for our particular relationship and the words in the card were so apt. I felt like a schoolgirl again. This was ridiculous . . . I was sixty years old!

As our time together passed that weekend, I began to have a sneaking feeling that Owen was a little arrogant and self—opinionated. On the other hand, he was kind, caring. He was obviously a conscientious and hard worker and had most of the ethical values I cherished. We had so much in common. We spoke easily of our late spouses, our children, our work. Apart from holding hands, there was no physical intimacy between us. Owen was obviously on his guard after our telephone conversation where I had stated the parameters to our relationship so emphatically.

When I got into bed that night, I thanked God for helping me through our first meeting. I felt he was a very pleasant person. Though I was attracted to Owen physically, I couldn't see this relationship developing into anything more than a good friendship. I didn't believe anyone could love me.

Once the weekend was over, I was certain I wouldn't hear from him again. I was wrong. Owen's phone calls came through almost every day. Even when I went back to South Africa to visit my family, he phoned me daily. My mother told me she would really like to see me getting married again and settling down. To this day, her words still resound in my ears, "Angie, you will make someone a good wife! You have got so much to offer. Please don't close yourself off. Let God lead and guide you. Allow yourself to be happy again. You are still young.

Owen's phone calls only seemed to complicate the emotions I was feeling. One evening, when he phoned, Mum answered and called me to the phone. When I had finished the call, she said, "Angie, that man seems very keen on you. He has phoned you just about every day since you've been home. How can you possibly know he's not for you if you don't give him a chance? Get to know him better. Meet him again." I brushed her off saying that, if the relationship was meant to be, it would sort itself out. I was certainly not going to run after him or try to make things happen. It wasn't long after this that Mum died, but those words of hers kept coming back to me.

I had decided I would go to live in England for the time being. Throwing myself into my caring work, I had little time to dwell on my personal situation. It helped me deal with the deep sadness of losing Mum. During that time, I hadn't had time to grieve over my great loss. I returned to South Africa almost a year later and only then did the full impact of Mum's death hit me. It was during that time that I got closure about my loss. God showed me I had been a good daughter to her and always honoured and loved her. I had nothing to regret about my wonderful relationship I had shared with Mum. I had everything to thank and praise God for in both her life and in her death. I miss her physical presence and companionship, but know we will be together again forever. That is my great comfort.

Owen's phone calls never stopped. Our discussions ranged through a whole gamut of subjects, both light and of a much deeper variety. We were able to communicate freely and easily on any subject, that was, until Owen broached the subject of sex! I almost swallowed my tongue. I cautiously entered the discussion and gradually began to feel more comfortable as we discussed other sensitive issues of our pasts, our previous marriages and our children. I have always been a very private person and I certainly wasn't prepared to discuss the intimate aspects of my previous marriage with Owen. I believed that was sacrosanct territory. We discussed our relationships with God, married life in broad, general terms, what marriage was in His sight and what His pre-requisites for marriage were.

I had been talking on the phone to Owen for two and a half years when people started teasing me and asking, "How is your romance going?" "It's not a romance. It's just a friendship," I would answer. When they asked whether I thought it would ever lead to a something deeper, my answer was always a resounding "No!" Their constant questions, however, did get me thinking. They were right to prod me about our relationship and I had to ask myself where the friendship was going. I was working in Dorchester at the time. Mum's words kept coming back to me. I made up my mind to challenge Owen with that question when he next called.

I lost all diplomacy when I spoke to him and just blurted it out, "Owen, where do you think this friendship is going? I want you to know that I am not here to fill your lonely gap. I certainly don't intend being your telephone friend for the rest of my life!" There was complete stunned silence on the other end of the phone. Owen had never expected that to come from me. I was shocked at my having had the courage to voice the question.

For once, Owen was at a loss for words. After a silence, he said, "I don't know how to answer that. I can tell you I am not using you to fill my lonely gap. I don't want you to be my telephone friend only and really do want to see you again." Now I was the one stunned into silence. I made an excuse and quickly told him I had to go. My charge was ringing for me.

I went to bed that night questioning myself about my foolish behaviour and pleading with God to get me out of the mess I'd got myself into. My head was flooded with such a jumble of thoughts as I lay there for about an hour, imagining all sorts of outcomes to the situation I'd stirred up.

When, the next two nights, Owen phoned, he didn't mention that disastrous conversation at all. I have since discovered that Owen is a very deep thinker and the conversation was never far from his mind at that time. I have also discovered he loves to surprise me. Three days later, he phoned and announced he would be down for the weekend. He had booked into a local bed-and-breakfast in Dorchester and asked if I could arrange to get some time off. He had caught me off my guard and had really called my bluff. He would be with me three days later! Was I ready for this? What was I getting myself into? The family I worked for were so wonderful and were delighted at the news. They told me to go ahead with my plans and they would sort themselves out. I couldn't believe this was all happening so fast.

The Friday arrived! I had bathed and changed and was ready when Owen rang the bell. My heart pounding, I could once again feel myself blushing deep scarlet. I opened the front door and looked into his lovely, blue, kind eyes. I knew without a shadow of doubt this man was going to be a permanent part of my life. My tummy was filled with a flight of butterflies! After introducing him to Edwina, I had to excuse myself and rushed to the bathroom. "Pull yourself together, girl! You are not a teenager. Why are you letting this get to you like this?" I splashed my florid face with cold water. What was happening to me? I hadn't felt this way for years. I certainly hadn't expected to be overcome by puppy love again at my age.

I emerged from the bathroom, feeling slightly less flustered. We walked down the road to the local pub for dinner. I could talk more easily now. Once we were seated, I felt I'd better say what I had to say before my courage deserted me. Out it all poured! "I don't know what you see in me. I'm not like the sexy, slim ladies you have probably dated before. I have got so much baggage what with my son being an addict and with all the business commitments I am still having to honour." Owen smiled. He took my hand, "Angela, Angela stop! Give me a chance to answer you." Nonplussed, I said, "Okay." Looking straight into my eyes, he asked, "Do you know you have the most beautiful eyes?" Oh, my goodness! I blushed even more violently. After so many years, I wasn't used to receiving compliments, especially from a man.

"Angela, I want nothing from you but for you to let me love you, protect you and care for you! I've known about all about your baggage for two and a half years. You've told me all about it and it doesn't worry me in the least. Everyone has a certain amount of baggage. Please will you think about it?" I was shattered, "I really don't know what to say to you, but, yes, I will think about it." We enjoyed such a wonderful evening together. For the first time in years, I felt so very special and cherished. As Owen walked me home with his strong caring arm around my shoulder, I felt so secure and happy. We stopped along the way and he asked me if he could kiss me. Everything felt so right. It was wonderful. The words "I do love you, Owen," tumbled out of my mouth. He stared at me wide-eyed. I was startled at myself for having said it. I had always found expressing my emotions verbally very difficult. He dropped me off at the house, and returned to his bed-and-breakfast for the night.

I was elated. I was feeling soaring emotions I had never thought possible. I really loved this man. How could it be? I hardly knew him, apart from our telephone friendship and our brief weekends together. Owen called for me the next morning for a visit to an air museum. Having been a pilot in the South African Air Force, aeroplanes were of great interest to him. If I were being honest, I was convinced I'd be bored. But, in this special man's company, I thoroughly enjoyed the museum. It was an exhilaratingly wonderful day we spent together. Again that evening, Owen took me out to dinner. In every way, the weekend was truly amazing. Before he left on the Sunday, he arrived at my door with a large bouquet of the most beautiful flowers for me. They were in anticipation of Valentine's Day the following Tuesday. He was keen for me to meet his children and so we arranged that I would go to Manchester for three days before returning to South Africa for my daughter's birthday.

By the time I reached Manchester, I was almost overcome with nerves! I was assailed with doubts about how I would manage now that I was on Owen's home turf. I was to be staying in his home, being inspected by his family in a totally unfamiliar territory! How would I manage? I felt completely inadequate. I needn't have. Owen was an absolute gentleman in every respect and made negotiating every new aspect of the whole weekend so easy. Every evening, he and I prayed together, thanking God for each other and asking Him to help us to do things His way.

The day before I left, Owen said he had to go into town to attend to a few matters and needed to pop into a jeweller's to get a new battery for his watch. Without wasting a moment as we walked into the shop, he announced to the assistant, "We would like to buy an engagement ring." "Yes, Sir" she replied, bringing out a tray of rings. I was flabbergasted. After all, this was a second marriage. I hadn't been expecting anything like this. I was overcome with embarrassment and really didn't know where to put myself! I have always hated being the centre of attraction and felt, there in the jeweller's, all eyes were on me. Owen smiled so reassuringly, "Pick any ring you'd like." I felt a great rush of gratitude to the shop assistant who was so considerate, as she helped me choose a lovely solitaire diamond ring.

Such an air of unreality swirled around me but, Owen slipped that ring onto my finger, a peace settled in my heart and I knew everything about what was happening was right. It was as the Lord had planned it.

We both felt such a wrenching when I had to fly back to South Africa the next day. The three weeks apart which lay ahead were going to be very difficult. The time we had just spent together had been so deliriously happy.

Owen phoned me every day whilst I was away. The time with my family was very special but I missed him desperately. He was at Gatwick airport to meet me on my return. We drove back to Manchester together.

When we had first got engaged, our plan had been that we would be married in December in South Africa. We had changed our minds because of family considerations. Now, we had decided, Owen's children would celebrate with us in England. We then would celebrate with my family in December in South Africa where we planned to spend Christmas. With those plans in mind, we decided to bring the date of our wedding forward. We had no reason to wait. We arranged to meet with the vicar who would marry us. The date of the ceremony was set. I knew I was the most blessed woman alive.

Owen took care of all the details of our special day . . . the bookings for my hair and nail appointments, the service at the church, the hotel where the reception was to be held and all the flowers. It was exhilarating having this capable man taking charge and making all the decisions. When I asked him what I could do to help, his reply was, "I know you will look beautiful on the day. All you have to do is to make sure you get to the church."

I went back to work in Dorchester. Edwina advised me where to shop for my wedding outfit. She was very excited at being involved. She was most specific about what sort of outfit I needed to wear. As red was Owen's favourite colour for me to wear, I chose a stunning dress and matching jacket in red with ivory accessories. My charge beamed with approval as she made me parade in the outfit I had chosen. "Angela, that is most appropriate and tasteful my dear! You couldn't have made a finer choice." I was thrilled that I had met her exacting standards.

We both wept as we rehearsed our marriage vows the Tuesday evening before the ceremony. They seemed so much more solemn and meaningful than they had when we had spoken them so many years earlier at our first marriages. That evening, we chatted for ages about the vast differences between marrying for the first time as young people and the implications we faced in this our second marriage.

The one deep sadness I had to deal with was that I was not going to have Mum, my children or my siblings with us on our special day. I was thrilled, however, that all my English family had replied they would be celebrating our happy event with us.

The Friday before the wedding, Owen asked me to come for a drive with him to collect a parcel which was being delivered at the airport. I really didn't want to go as I had so much to do that day, but I reasoned that the drive would be a good time to relax and chat with Owen.

When we got to the airport, the plane had not landed yet and so we settled in the airport lounge to have a drink. Suddenly, Owen got up saying the plane had landed. As we stood at Arrivals, I caught a glimpse of a familiar face . . . I saw my daughter Lisa coming through the doors towards me. I was convinced I was hallucinating! I let out a scream of joy and ran to her. How everyone had managed to keep this wonderful surprise a secret was incredible!

Owen had arranged for Lisa and me to spend the night before our wedding at the local hotel and the two of us spent a very special 'girlie time' together. Lisa used the time to give me some 'tips' which she felt I needed with my having been single for almost seven years! "Mum" she said firmly, "I hope you have a nice nightdress? You do know you are going to have to sleep with Owen once you are married." I felt acutely awkward and embarrassed at my eldest daughter lecturing me about 'the birds and the bees'! We alternated between laughing and crying so much that evening. It was wonderful having my precious daughter with me at such a momentous time in my life.

The great day dawned. To the strains of the organ playing "Amazing Grace", my cousin Jonathan walked me down the aisle. God's wonderful grace had brought two people so far from the same distant land to a strange country for them to meet and fall in love. It was a day of great joy and the Lord blessed every detail to perfection.

I lay awake on our wedding night marvelling at the truly amazing way in which so many aspects of our two lives had worked to bring us to this day of all days. I remembered that God in His Word says that He does all things well. He works all things together for the good of those who love him. I had never dared imagine I could ever love anyone in this way again. But, here I was loving this special man and he loving me. Rediscovering love is a promise for all those who feel they have lost it.

Chapter 16

MY OTHER SECRETS OF SURVIVAL

My life's journey with its landmark heartaches and joys has been sign-posted with clearly marked choices. I have had to make critical decisions which have led me to overcome and to ultimately survive. Hidden deep in some of my greatest disappointments, I found invaluable treasures which have radically transformed my life and mapped out a totally different future for me. I feel strongly that many people avoid the difficult choices on their journey. They abandon the possibility of a richer future too easily. Without earnestly searching, they miss the solution to what they are facing which lies just around the corner.

When we fail we do not automatically become a failure. We do when we quit. Failure is a vital part of the journey of learning. Winston Churchill said, "I've never failed at anything in my life. I was simply given another opportunity to get it right."

To every challenge there is always a solution. It may not necessarily take the form we feel it should. Sometimes it will require us to test various options offered. We need to embrace the opportunities that come our way. Without doing so, we will never know the sweet taste of success.

The father of the motor industry, Henry Ford, was a man who made mistakes, but he persevered and ultimately succeeded. When he built his first car, he forgot to fit it with a reverse gear. He went into bankruptcy five times on his way up. He was driven by determination and refused to give up, no matter how the problems appeared to be.

Even when things seem so tough that no solution is obvious, a way can be found, with perseverance and persistence. Whenever I find myself in impossible situations, I always remind myself that, if I was able to push through and succeed yesterday, I can again today and I certainly will be able to again tomorrow.

I have learned through the traumatic experiences I have had to go through that God has a plan for my life and a purpose through my pain. I was never able to see it until I summonsed the courage to surrender my pain, fear, self—pity and despair to Him. Every painful experience in my life has had a lesson to teach me when I have been open to learn. I have always questioned things and never just accepted situations. What could I learn from the situation? What was the all wise, all loving God trying to teach me? How was He trying to help me? Would the situation make me a bitter or better person? Could the circumstances add value to mine or someone else's life?

There have been times when I have questioned strongly why yet again I was being put through another testing trial. I have realised life does not work to suit my time schedule. Being made to wait has been a stark reminder to me that I am not the one in charge. Often, there would be no obvious reason why God has delayed giving me the answers I had asked for. I quickly came to understand that He was under no obligation to conform His ways and timing to mine. Learning to wait develops patience, a strength I grew in over many years. I have been enormously humbled through the whole process but have also been greatly rewarded. When I look back on my life, there has never been anything that I've been through, good or bad, that has been a waste of time or hasn't ultimately worked out for my good in every detail . . . so I'm prepared to wait.

Most of the lessons I've learned have actually helped others more than they have helped me. Being unselfish and holding all things lightly is a definite requisite for someone to live to the fullest measure designed for them, but it comes with a price. The demands of other people's lives and their problems and needs have cost me my time, energy and effort and finances. I have been willing to give all these freely. Most people can't be bothered about becoming involved in other people's situations, especially if there's no personal gain for them. The truth I have seen at close range is that it is definitely more blessed to give than to receive.

Over the years, I have discovered first-hand the difference a simple phone-call or visit has made to a person going through a difficult time. It has made them feel loved and assured them they are not alone and gave them new hope. Often, when I've been exhausted or found myself going through a particularly difficult time in my own life, I have discovered that to be the best time to consider others' needs. In no time at all after having contacted them, having spent quality time listening to and talking with them, I have realised that I have taken the focus off myself. An amazing by-product of this is that I too feel uplifted and encouraged. Thinking of and caring for others when I have had a need myself, has always carried a twofold benefit . . . in helping others I have ended up helping myself. It works every time.

When I've considered others' spiritual, emotional or physical needs before my own, I have been amazed at how all my own needs seem to have been met automatically. The law of 'sowing and reaping' has come into effect and never fails. Genesis 8:22 reads, "While the earth remains, seed time and harvest shall not cease." We all have something to give . . . a smile, a word of encouragement, a helping hand, a prayer, the gift of oneself.

Each person who comes across my path is special. They are worthy of being respected, helped and loved. A poet once wrote, "Love in your heart is not put there to stay. Love isn't love till you give it away." People are able to cope with being rejected by many, so long as they have a safe place they can call 'home' where they know they can come and be loved by someone else. When I have been beaten and almost crushed by life in general or by my job, my finances or even by my family and friends, my home has been my sanctuary where I have felt totally accepted and loved.

I have always ensured that my home was my haven. It has been a place to run to from the tempests and trials of life. This safe refuge has been a place set apart where I have been able to feel safe, to love and to be loved. It's been where I have been able to relax, unwind, laugh and enjoy my loved ones, be supported and support others. My home has been my place of restoration. There, I have been able to be recharged by love and acceptance. There I have found strength and peace and been made ready to face the future.

Even during our most difficult financial situations, my first priority, after giving to God, has been to pay the rent, electricity, water and groceries bills at the beginning of each month. Showing integrity in honouring my debts has protected my haven and has ensured that it has always been available for both me and my family to escape to. Even the most meagre meal has been made special when the table has been laid with nice linen, crockery and cutlery. It was in the most difficult times that I took special care to have candles on the table and fresh flowers from my garden to make the home warm and welcoming to both family and friends. These were such precious family times. No matter what food was on the table, we kept our dignity and treasured having each other.

I am now sixty-four years old. I have never gone hungry nor have I not found a way either through or out of every difficult situation. It may sound harsh to say that most lonely people are selfish people. A person who cares for others is rarely ever lonely. The greatest cure for loneliness is to live for and be there for others. I can honestly say I have never been lonely. I have felt alone many times because of circumstances which come with my occupation, especially when I am working in the countryside. I am grateful for modern technology. I have always had my mobile phone, computer or a landline to keep in contact with my family and friends. I have discovered the radio and, more especially, my Christian Praise and Worship music are great distractions and are so uplifting when I am alone or things have become painfully quiet. To listen to and to be caught up in Praise and Worship during those stormy times brings wisdom, peace and calm to any situation.

The greatest gift I believe I have been blessed with is to have always been open and teachable. There is nothing worse than a know-all. Many times, I have found myself surrounded by brilliant people and feeling myself a real ignoramus. I have learnt that, unless I really know what I'm talking about, to keep my mouth shut and to listen. Until I do talk, these very clever people have no idea of what I do or don't know. Though many of us like to think we know it all, there are none who do. There is always something new to be learnt, no matter how simple or practical it may be, if we are good listeners. A still tongue definitely makes a wise head. In the most volatile situations, it was my silence which often spoke far louder than any words I could have said. In some of the most difficult situations I have faced, particularly with my children, people have known exactly what my silence has been communicating.

I have often been aware of my family thinking, "Angela's really dumb. She's not as smart as us. Perhaps she's even a bit simple." I know how they think and I am happy for them to think that way about me but, all the time, I am listening very carefully. I am gleaning all I can. I am weighing the whole situation up, deciding whether it's even worth bothering to vocalise an opinion or thought. Often, I've learned so much more from just listening than I would have had I spoken a single word.

Many people mistake my meekness for weakness. Nothing could be further from the truth. It takes extreme strength, self-control, humility, gentleness, and caring to be genuinely meek. I've learned, through many years of being a part of a large family who are all more intellectual than I am and who are competitive and controlling and that meekness is an invaluable tool for me to deal with them.

The stumbling blocks in my own character have been many and chief among them were insecurity and a sense of rejection. They held me captive for many years. I was the only one who could remove these obstacles. My traumatic start in life had ensured that my parents were my only form of security as I grew up. I was terrified of change or of trying anything new. Today, I stand in absolute amazement at the many changes I have embraced in the last few years and at how my confidence and self-acceptance have grown immeasurably. My family find it hard to credit the growth in me. It's been wonderful journey for me. I can say with total conviction that life began for me at sixty.

There can be no real retirement for someone who is God's child. I came to realise this fact so very late in my life and now at my age I accept that He can and probably will send me wherever and whenever He chooses, no matter what the season of my life. I'm not seeking status accorded by people. I do know I will earn the right kind of status which really counts by being of service to others. I don't have to promote or protect myself. He does it for me. What rest and peace I find in that assurance!

I only began to trust and feel more secure when I really understood the intimate nature of my relationship with God. With Christ in me, He began to teach me the true meaning of leaning on Him entirely and finding my security in Him as He allowed me to go through the various experiences of my life. The Lord has let experience be my teacher. Sometimes it has been a very harsh mentor, but it has nonetheless taught me very valuable lessons in the schoolhouse of life.

Without God, there is no security in jobs, religion, relationships, health, possessions or positions anywhere in this world. All of these can be lost or change overnight. When I am in need of help or guidance, I bind my will to the Father's perfect will and my mind to the mind of Christ. I then loose myself of all the fears and insecurities.

The technique of binding and loosing I learned from scripture, "I will give you the keys to the kingdom of Heaven. Whatever you bind on earth has already been bound in Heaven, and whatever you loose on earth has already been loosed in Heaven." (Matthew 16:19). It is so simple yet so practical and effective. It took me years to really practise God's presence in each and every situation in life. He always shows me a way where there has seemed to be no way.

True happiness rests in having a purpose in life. Queen Esther knew her purpose in life, under the guidance of her uncle Mordecai. He prepared her to be able to move into the purpose and destiny God had for her. In the same way today, Christ and His Holy Spirit in us prepare and guide us to fulfil our purpose in this life. Because I have been prepared to let the Lord prepare me for my future through all the times of testing in my life, I have never been happier than I am now at this time in my life. I've never been freer and more at peace than I am now. The love of money and possessions has changed so many people around me and not given them any real peace or freedom. It changed me once and it certainly wasn't for the better. I thank God that through His forgiveness and grace I was able to leave that time behind. I have more freedom now than I ever had when I owned property, a business, expensive cars and all the luxuries I ever thought I needed or wanted. Now, my needs are so minimal . . . that's so much less to worry about! I believe most people could have won medals in the Art of Worrying. Worry can have such a stranglehold in our lives and can destroy our capacity to live in the wonder and wealth of the present moment. People are far too focused on the future. Their entire being is trapped by thoughts of what might go wrong. Their gratitude for and enjoyment of the present is tainted by this obsession. Entrusting myself and my troubles and needs to God is my single sure defence against worry.

I have total confidence in the plans God has for me as I walk in His will. I may not always be comfortable in a particular situation but I am convinced that, ultimately, it will work out because He's in charge. He ensures that I am never short of work and that I meet the nicest people. Boosting my financial equity is not the most important issue of my life . . . the lives and needs of others are my priority.

God's track record for meeting my every need, protecting me, leading and guiding me is perfect and always on time. I've never had one challenge come my way where He has let me down. I am grateful that He has always met my needs according to His perfect will and not my permissive, stubborn and selfish will.

The greatest of the keys to real happiness is to know God personally and intimately. Other keys of great importance are having a close, loving family, good friends and having a sense of purpose and direction for one's life and faithfully pursuing them. I discovered that the key to success in my workplace was that I should let my vocation become my vacation . . . I do what I love and love what I do. I've never been one to just sit idly by, waiting for things somehow just to happen. But if I have prayed about the issue of the moment and have felt God leading me and have had a peace because of that, then I have been quite content to allow things to happen as I know God has planned them.

Close behind insecurity and the debilitating sense of rejection on my list of weaknesses were pride and perfectionism, a pair which go hand in hand. As far back as I can remember, I always felt compelled to do things perfectly. I still feel more comfortable knowing I have done things as they should be. The difference is that now, I try not to foist my standards onto others. I have learned to be able to tell the difference between when things need to be perfectly done and when they don't. In the past, I would insist that everything had to be done my way and according to my timing. But I had to learn some lessons the hard way. I realised my impatience was caused by my pride. Impatience could only be driven out by patience. Thankfully, I have grown to be far more patient and tolerant of others who do not behave or accomplish things to the standards I expect of myself. This has been a tough lesson and it took me a long time to learn. I can't imagine where I found the arrogance to think that I could change people, their lives or their habits. I have grown to never point an accusing finger at another person for anything I have excused in myself. I have hated seeing faults and character traits in my own children that I recognised in myself. To my great sorrow, I realise now that I was at my very worst as a perfectionist with my late husband and my own children. Now I can see God's sense of humour in giving me my laid-back family. Their attitude to life was diametrically opposed to mine.

My 'Martyr Syndrome' performances could have won me many Oscars . . . I so often gave in to my sense of self-pity. Through these dramatic productions of mine, my family remained relaxed and enjoyed life as it came to them. I was utterly miserable as I allowed myself to be robbed as I gave in to stress and anger. Eventually, it dawned on me that my anger was also a bitter fruit of my pride. My anger gripped me in a stranglehold when the family wouldn't cooperate with me or perform as I felt they should. I was always consumed with concern about people's opinions about me and my family. What a waste of emotional and physical energy! It is such pride to constantly demanding perfection in oneself and in others. That perfection will never be found in any man or woman and it is foolish to look for it or to demand. Now I can rejoice in being able to accept myself just as I am. Those close to me are also able to be happy to see me free in that self-acceptance. That's true freedom!

It must have been plain through my story that forgiveness has so often been an enormous hurdle for me to get over. C.S. Lewis said, "Everyone thinks forgiveness is a lovely idea until they have to forgive someone." When we hang onto unforgiveness, we are bound to the situation which caused us hurt and pain. We can never be free of it. The memory of the pain attached to the situation pursues us relentlessly. Unforgiveness is a very natural human emotion . . . forgiveness is supernatural.

It is crucial that we learn to forgive others . . . we also need to learn to forgive ourselves . . . just like those who hurt us, we are not perfect. Many do not understand that we also need to not hold grudges against God for the things in our lives that happen or don't happen according to our plans. Many times, when I was the injured party, I struggled with being able to forgive the one who had offended me. I tried to justify to myself that the person didn't deserve my forgiveness. After much inward debate, justifying why I shouldn't forgive them, the Holy Spirit reminded me of how God's forgiveness towards me is His greatest acts of love. He demands that I forgive others as an expression of extreme, self-sacrificing love towards them. I am so grateful that He gives me the grace to forgive them and the ability to see them through His eyes. Unforgiveness, bitterness and holding grudges are like a cancer . . . they cause such inescapable pain and imprison us. Forgiveness is the laser treatment that burns away the pain.

More often than not, I have known that I could not wait for the offender to make the first move towards me so there could be forgiveness and healing. Often, it has been obvious that they probably would never make the move. It was up to me. I had to be the first to forgive even if I could only express my forgiveness to God . . . sometimes, the situation was so severe and the other person was completely unapproachable. Often, they were totally unaware that I had forgiven them. But God did and I knew that He knew. He was then able to take me to the next level and into greater degrees of freedom.

In forgiving those who had injured me didn't mean admitting that what they had done was right. It was telling myself and God that, no matter what had been done to me, I was choosing to release myself from the hurt attached to the words spoken or deeds perpetrated against me. I ask God to forgive those responsible. I also ask Him to forgive me for any way in which I may have contributed towards the situation. I then know I am free. Whether they ever apologise or acknowledge their wrong-doing, I choose to release them. Whenever I am reminded of what was done to me or said about me, I immediately take those thoughts captive and give them to the Lord. I make a choice to let God deal with the people in His way. He knows far more deeply than I ever possibly can . . . and He loves them like I will never be able to.

Perhaps forgiving oneself for wrong doing is far more difficult than forgiving others. Making wrong choices, speaking idle words, indulging any of our weaknesses, trying to control or manipulate situations out of fear instead of trusting God, choosing not to invoke His help and guidance puts us in situations where we need forgive ourselves. I had a revelation of the liberating truth found in Scripture in 1 John Chapter 1:9, "if we confess our sins, He is faithful and righteous to forgive us our sins and cleanse us from all our unrighteousness". It took years of practising what this particular passage counselled before it became a natural and habitual part of my everyday living.

There was a long time in my life, even in my early days as a Christian, when I struggled with great dissatisfaction . . . I would moan, grumble and complain. I would blame God for the loss of a loved one, for a family problem, for an accident and for the general stresses and burdens I experienced in everyday living. I have since learned to do as Paul teaches in 1 Thessalonians 5:16-18, "Rejoice always; pray without ceasing; in everything give thanks; for this is the will of God in Christ Jesus for you." I remember reading something written by a missionary, "Do not go to sleep at night until you have counted ten things for which to thank God." I believe it is such wise advice from a humble servant of God.

Many agnostics, intellectuals, and self-sufficient, successful people in the world's eyes have asked me, "Angela, if God loves you so much and is in control of things as you say He is, why have you gone through so many terrible experiences and so much pain in your life?" I do not have a pat answer to that question. Christianity is certainly not a magic wand that can be waved to make one rich, happy and healthy. I can only share my personal experience of a loving, merciful God who has never abandoned me in any of those experiences. He has always brought me through each of them. He has enabled me to be much stronger, more loving, more patient and compassionate to others because I have known the pain of brokenness and loss. I can empathise with them and truthfully say to them, "I know how you feel!" Jesus told His disciples they too would go through hardships. If we are his disciples, why should we expect to be exempt from trials and testings? He told His disciples in Luke 9:23-25, "If anyone desires to come after me, let him deny himself, and take up his cross daily and follow me. For whosoever desires to save his life will lose it, but whoever loses his life for my sake will save it. For what does it profit a man if he gains the whole world, and is himself destroyed or lost?"

I have lived through many seasons of struggle, brokenness, dryness and pain. These seasons have always been followed by ones of peace, healing, restoration, refreshment and, most importantly, by joy . . . a joy that the world could never have given me. Each season has had a God-ordained purpose which has ultimately brought about good in my life. I will, no doubt, experience many more good and bad seasons in the years to come. Thankfully, I have great peace in knowing I have real security in every circumstance. That peace comes from the greatest source . . . from the only one who I know will never let me down. My challenge is that God should be given the chance to show His incredible faithfulness. There is nothing to be lost and everything to be gained. A relationship with Him will take time, commitment, effort and sensitivity to develop. With Christ in my life, I now enjoy and live the best in this world. I also know I can expect to enjoy and live the best in the world to come. It is in embracing this certain promise and hope that assurance of eternal survival comes!